TWENTIETH CENTURY SERIES

Selected works of lasting significance.

DOUGLAS W. HOUSTON, LYMAN H. LEGTERS,
PETER H. MERKL, EDITORS

No. 1. German National Socialism,
1919-1945, *Martin Broszat*

No. 2. We Survived. Histories of the
Hidden and Hunted of Nazi Germany,
Eric H. Boehm

GERMAN NATIONAL SOCIALISM,

1919-1945

Martin Broszat

Translated from the German

by

KURT ROSENBAUM
Associate Professor of History
West Virginia University

and

INGE PAULI BOEHM
Assistant Editor
Historical Abstracts

CLIO PRESS
Santa Barbara, California

GERMAN NATIONAL SOCIALISM, 1919-1945

A translation of Martin Broszat's
**Der Nationalsozialismus. Weltanschauung,
Programm und Wirklichkeit** (National
Socialism. Philosophy, Program and
Reality), Stuttgart: Deutsche Verlags-
Anstalt, 1960

Library of Congress Card Number 66-26137

Grateful acknowledgment is made to James S. Beddie, the late Hilton Goss, Peter Merkl, Gerta H. Schaffner and Ellen A. Wakefield for the contributions they made toward making this a meaningful English translation.

Kurt Rosenbaum and Inge P. Boehm

CONTENTS

Preface

Discussions involving the Nazi dictatorship invariably raise the question: how could such a brutal system take hold in Germany? There are numerous works which explore this question. Some seek the roots of Nazism in Germany's past as far back as Luther; others analyze in detail the political situation in Germany just before Hitler was appointed chancellor. Since 1945 memoirs have been published, written by many of the men who held positions of power in the Third Reich, and diaries and recollections of those who opposed the regime. Dr. Martin Broszat has drawn on all of these sources and his book is an analysis based on the evidence which has become available since 1945, when Hitler's regime ended.

Broszat is a research associate of the Institut für Zeitgeschichte (Institute for Recent History) in Munich, which has been doing most of the significant research on Nazi Germany. His careful research is reflected in a number of monographs and articles on National Socialism, published by the Institute. Broszat has a well-earned reputation for being an expert on the Nazi period.

Broszat's book *Der Nationalsozialismus*, here translated, provides a concise analysis of the antecedents of the Nazi era, of the intellectual and emotional atmosphere of the Weimar Republic. He describes the motives and the hopes which led German conservatives and nationalists to support Hitler. Broszat shows how Hitler took advantage of the numerous political trends among the opponents of the democratic Weimar Republic in order to gain their votes and achieve control of Germany's government. Once power had been seized the gains were consolidated and the nation was hypnotized and terrorized. Those who had despised the unstable young democracy and who longed for the creation of a well-disciplined new state, but one socially conscious and attuned to German traditions, found that the romanticism which had motivated them was eliminated. A totalitarian state emerged.

Kurt Rosenbaum

1. *Introduction*

by PETER MERKL

Nearly half a century has passed since the rise of the Nazi Party in Germany; more than two decades ago it collapsed along with the shattered German war machine. Yet National Socialism remains as enigmatic and controversial as ever. Its legions of ghosts and skeletons will not remain buried in the trash bin of history. Who were these men who would not rest until they had erected the most hideous dictatorship on earth and plunged the world into the Second World War? What did they want and what did their supporters see in them? How could a highly civilized nation fall for the siren song of a Hitler and identify itself with him to the bitter end?

In the last decade, a number of penetrating scholarly monographs have been written by a new generation of West German historians on the origins and the internal dynamics of the Third Reich. These have only in small part been made available in English. The distinguished Munich *Institut für Zeitgeschichte* (Institute of Recent History), of which the author of this short volume is a research associate, has been in the forefront of separating fact from fancy about the Third Reich. Much of the recent historical research published in Europe, including other writings of Broszat, still awaits translation.

To appreciate Broszat's *Der Nationalsozialismus,* the English-speaking reader must remember that this book was written by a German historian for a German audience. Considering the complexity of the subject, it is very important to bear in mind what the author chose not to undertake. The book makes no attempt to supply the broad frame of reference which readers have come to expect of a historical work about a foreign country. Except for the chronology supplied by one of the translators, Dr. Rosenbaum, and the biographic sketches at the end, the reader is presumed to be familiar with the sequence of situations and events of recent German history. In concentrating on the *völkisch*[1] groups up to the year 1929 from

---

[1]*Völkisch is derived from* Volk, *meaning people. The word has the same origins as the English "folk," and shares its overtones of an egalitarian populism and a highly integrated, homogeneous, ethnic community. "Völkisch" is used to describe the German extreme rightist movements and radical splin-*

which the Nazi movement sprang, for example, the author expects the reader to know that he is not describing the climate of public opinion of the Weimar Republic at large but only a small, self-contained part of it. The vote of the *völkisch* groups, including the Nazi movement, was around one to two percent throughout most of the Weimar elections. In the year of the great inflation and of the struggle between the French occupation of the Ruhr area and a nationalist underground 1923/1924, the *völkisch* vote suddenly rose to seven per cent. With the mass unemployment and bankruptcies of the Great Depression, the Nazi and *völkisch* vote gathered strength rapidly, this time to a peak of nearly half the electorate in little more than three years. It was precisely this crisis character of the Nazi landslide of the years 1930-1932 which led some American social scientists to look for the "crisis strata" of German society at the time, voters

ter groups whose most significant characteristic was their opposition to the Western tradition - often to capitalism -, to the democratic and republican ideas of the Weimar Republic, and especially to any foreign policy which meant German adjustment to the consequences of defeat in World War I or to international conciliation in general. They emphasized anti-Semitism and anti-Catholicism. They saw the differences of man as more significant than their common ties. They promoted concepts of "race" and "blood," the superiority of the Germanic people over the Slavs or other neighboring ethnic elements. They represented a rightist opposition to the Enlightenment and the West European heritage of the French Revolution. Their chauvinism and extreme nationalism is sometimes used for the translation "chauvinist" or "nationalist," for lack of any better word. The inadequacy of these words leads us to retain the original völkisch.

who had not been *völkisch* or Nazi-oriented before
but were so vulnerable to economic crisis that they
panicked at the thought of another great inflation.

Broszat's book does not concern itself with the
"crisis strata" and their motivation, nor with the
vast political majority until the landslide occurred,
the political forces that guided and opposed the
democratic republic. Thus it also leaves aside another
fruitful line of inquiry of other historians, to find out
the political weaknesses and irreconcilable divisions
which according to many serious scholars ruined
Weimar democracy even before Hitler's movement
presented a serious challenge to it. Dr. Broszat
instead concentrates the searching focus of this study
on the question: What was "the character and essence
of National Socialism?" All the questions he raises
and answers are aimed at this elusive problem of
interpretation.

Broszat's interpretation is not the first attempt at
understanding the "essence" of National Socialism.
There have been many others and, to some extent,
they complement each other as long as one does not
accept any single interpretation to the exclusion of
all others. Broszat's greatest contribution in this
book is, in fact, to show by implication the limitations
of any one grand interpretive scheme. He stresses
some stubborn facts and aspects that resist general-
ization. The most simple-minded interpretation of
Nazism, to give an example, is the Marxist thesis of
the Nazi seizure of power as a counterrevolution to
the proletarian march to power. Long refuted by
historians, this theory has its mirror image in the
belief of some spokesmen of the American right wing

that National Socialism was "socialistic." Broszat
shows how historical reality eludes both of these
self-serving simplifications. He demonstrates the
prevalence of the populistic "anti-capitalist longing"
among Nazis and *völkisch* groups especially in the
1920's and until the 1933 riots against chain stores
in some localities, where zealous followers wanted
to do away with these capitalistic institutions by
force. Yet he also shows the noticeable turn of Hitler
to the right since 1929 when the paperhanger from
Austria eagerly began to accept the accolades and
money of admirers among German big industry and
finance. The socialist strand in the Nazi movement is
likewise shown as a strong determinant until Hitler's
break with Otto Strasser in 1931, particularly in
North Germany. But here, too, the last shred of the
strand, the Nazi trade union wing, was suppressed
once Hitler was in power.

The Nazi party knew how to be all things to all men
prior to attaining office. Once in power, it also knew
how to sidetrack its creditors or how to make good
on promises to whole classes of supporters with
nothing more than a verbal token formula, a ceremonial
gesture, or a semantic promotion. Nazi Germany was
a showman's and an adman's paradise, a country of
well-crafted illusions for the gullible, whether they
were farmers, military men, nationalists or *völkisch*
romantics.

Broszat's brief volume is a brilliant essay on the
relation between theory and practice in National
Socialism. He begins by exploring what the Nazi
sympathizers and supporters of the early thirties
expected of the Third Reich and how their dreams of

corporativism, of a Germanic law reform, and a
Germanic social and political renaissance were mis-
carried in the crudest form. In passing, the deep
alienation from society, the cultural pessimism of the
völkisch intellectuals and, consequently, their wild
utopian expectations came to light. Broszat also tells
the little-known story of where the broad outlines of
Nazi ideology came from: not from a "German
tradition from Luther to Hitler", as one American
school of thought has insisted, but from very specific
sources, although the varied and complex strands of
German cultural history have left their imprint on
Nazi propaganda as much as on diametrically opposed
German movements. The sources of Nazi ideology,
according to Broszat, are 1) the superficial super-
patriotism and latent insecurity of the "national
bourgeoisie" of the pre-1914 decades; 2) the myth of
German superiority and mission, pervaded with an air
of cultural pessimism, as culled from the writings
of Lagarde, Langbehn, Gobineau and other popular
writers; 3) the hundreds of *völkisch* oriented intellectuals, publications, and bourgeois and student
groups which in the Weimar Republic emerged from
the lunatic fringe position of the pre-1914 anti-Semites
and pan-Germans to become the small but effective
launching pad of Hitler's movement. This and not
the writings of Fichte, Treitschke or Nietzsche—
all of which required considerable doctoring to fit
them into Nazi ideology—was the ideological basis of
Nazism.

Broszat goes on to show how these malodorous
fruits of German bourgeois culture became ripe for
the plucking by the wayward Austrian corporal. A

major role fell to the impact of defeat in the world
war, which seemed to lay bare raw nerves and lure
skeletons out of mental closets everywhere. The whole
world of bourgeois morality and established institutions and procedures, in particular, broke down,
exposing sheer greed, class struggle and exploitation,
and rank prejudice everywhere. Returning veterans
and their young sympathizers, moreover, formed
endless vigilante organizations, Free Corps, fighting
leagues (Kampfbünde) and party militias, such as the
Brownshirts and the Red Front, in which a new kind
of mobilized, egalitarian society in place of the
discredited one of class distinctions and privileges
appeared to rise. These were the aimless "eternal
marchers" whom Hitler skillfully harnessed before
the wagon of the völkisch ideology, thereby fashioning
a potent fighting organization unlike the older kind
of bourgeois-Biedermeier völkisch debating societies.

The author places the proper stress on Hitler's
extraordinary organizing skill and tactical and strategic genius in domestic politics—far less in foreign
policy where the gullibility of the governments of
the Western powers came to his aid. Like other fascist
would-be dictators, Hitler was deeply impressed by
the power of the Marxian-socialist movements. He
appreciated, in particular, Lenin's "organizational
weapon," the Bolshevik cadres of well-trained, professional revolutionaries who succeeded in seizing
power in Russia against overwhelming odds. Thus
organization and strategy were all-important to the
Nazi Führer, while ideology served merely as an
organizing device, a Big Lie, the details of which are
exchangeable at will. Broszat pictures Hitler as a

man who cannot take his party's theorists seriously
enough to read their works or entrust them with
major responsibility; a man who uses his own ideology
chiefly for sloganeering and for oratorical display,
a man inspired more by the myth of violence taught
by George Sorel and practiced by Benito Mussolini
than by any ideology including his own. And yet
Broszat also emphasizes the sinister passion which
was the one and only stable element in the flux of
Hitler's doctrines, his obsessive anti-Semitic mania,
the driving force from the days of his youth to the
monstrous "final solution" of the "Jewish problem"
in Europe.

The judgment of history on Hitler, as it emerges
from the Broszat book, is that he was a man cease-
lessly driven by this sinister passion and by his
monstrous ego. It was to satisfy his ego that he
craved to make himself dictator, to lord it over
aristocrats and the barons of industry, while millions
of German bourgeois voters and other fools in their
self-illusion worshipped him. It was in large part
literally in order to be able to call himself "the
greatest general of all time" that he started World
War II and pursued it to the bitter end. And it is the
grisly result of the sinister passion which remains
as his legacy to the present and future generations
to which all the perspective of history will never find
a lighter side. Nazi genocide of Jews, Slavs, gypsies
and the murder of the incurably ill is his ugly monu-
ment. His deeds stand as a warning to present and
coming generations, a warning of the destruction
and ultimately of the self-destruction emanating from
pathological hatred.

A Translation of

Martin Broszat's

DER **NATIONALSOZIALISMUS**

2. The
"True" National Socialism:
Myth and Reality

The years which have passed since the demise of the Hitler era in 1945 make it relatively simple for the contemporary historian to present reliable statements about the character and the essence of National Socialism. We are the heirs of huge collections of documents with irrefutable facts on the characteristics of National Socialism. Some details may still be lacking, but the over-all judgment is not likely to be altered.

In the 1920's and the early 1930's, the direction of National Socialism was as yet uncertain, but there was some evidence of its future course. Diverse

impulses and hopes, and conflicting ideological concepts made the characteristic ambiguity of the
National Socialist movement more pronounced. This
led observers to make the most divergent interpretations. The manifold and conflicting expectations of
National Socialism were expressed as late as the
spring of 1932, when Albrecht Erich Günther issued
a volume which was significantly entitled *Was wir
vom Nationalsozialismus erwarten* (What we expect
of National Socialism). In this book twenty well-
known persons from many walks of life—political
commentators, poets, writers, and jurists, Protestants and Catholics—interpreted the imminent seizure
of power by the National Socialists in these greatly
divergent ways: realization of the "German political
idea of the 20th century"; national education of the
people by commitment to the "depth of the *völkisch*
character" (Wilhelm Stapel); "reorganization of the
economy based on farming" and "construction of a
state which would guard its power abroad and protect
morality at home" (August Winnig); reawakening of
a "metaphysics of confidence" as the condition for
a new folk art (Hanns Johst); and the National
Socialist idea of *Volkstum* (folk, integral nationalism)
as a catalyst for a closer link of the professing
Protestant Christian with the Lutheran "molding of
character" (Pastor D. Forsthoff).

In these and similar ways the hopes of the men in
the national-conservative camp varied. The majority
of these individuals did not belong to the NSDAP
(Nationalsozialistische Deutsche Arbeiterpartei: The
National Socialist German Workers' Party). Setting

aside their doubts and misgivings, these conservatives cast their lot with Hitler because they believed that he would, in the end, help in the attainment of their young conservative, national-revolutionary and similar goals and endeavors. The widespread errors in the evaluation of National Socialism accompanied Hitler's seizure of power and made it possible. These errors were later also the source of disillusionment.

Oswald Spengler's political writings belong to this category of especially noteworthy involuntary intellectual services to National Socialism. Spengler was internationally famous as a philosopher of history and publicist. He became an outspoken intellectual opponent of the Weimar Republic, against which he leveled vitriolic attacks. His essay *Preussentum und Sozialismus* (Prussianism and Socialism), which appeared in the summer of 1919, had been one of the most effective initial intellectual signals for launching the counterrevolution then developing against the new Weimar democracy.

A few weeks after the National Socialist assumption of power, Oswald Spengler published his last political work entitled *Jahre der Entscheidung* (Years of Decision). He frankly confessed:

> "No one could have longed more for the national revolution of this year than I. I hated the filthy revolution of 1918 from its inception, as treason perpetrated by the second-rate among our people .... Everything I have written since then about politics was directed against the

powers which entrenched themselves, with the
aid of our enemies, on our mountain of misery
and misfortune. Every line was designed to
contribute to their overthrow and I hope that this
was the case. Something *had* to happen, in any
form, to liberate the deepest instincts in our
blood."

Spengler's satisfaction over the fall of the Weimar
Republic was already mixed with doubts and disappointments. The forceful regeneration for which he
had longed, and for the sake of which he had approved
and demanded the destruction of the past, was different from the reality of the first months of Nazi
(National Socialist) rule. He saw, instead of the hard
Prussian discipline of a modern Caesardom which
he had conjured up, a state swamped by the hetero-
geneous mass of the party followers, who saw in the
seizure of power primarily the due date for the
redemption of what they presumed to be their proper
reward. Spengler recognized the self-glorification in
the party propaganda for the masses, which aimed at
convincing the party and the people through torchlight
parades and rallies that a colossal victory had been
achieved on the "Day of the National Rebirth."
Spengler, who understood "race" to mean a human
and manly type who was formed through strict
upbringing and tradition, discovered that Hitler's
circle interpreted the theory of "race" in the most
primitive way, literally in a zoological manner. They
were competing in projects to breed a Nordic people

by biological selection. His first evaluation of the
Nazi assumption of power is therefore dominated by
pessimism:

> "This is no time or occasion for ecstasy and
> a sense of triumph. Woe to those who mistake
> mobilization for victory! This assumption of
> power took place in a whirlpool of strength and
> weakness. I notice with concern that it is daily
> celebrated with so much noise ... history is not
> sentimental and woe to him who takes himself
> sentimentally! ... Elements came to power who
> consider the enjoyment of power as the end result
> and who would like to make eternal a condition
> which is only momentarily acceptable. Sound
> ideas are exaggerated by fanatics to the point of
> self-dissolution. A great promise in the beginning
> ends in a tragedy or comedy."

In the following years Spengler spoke out with
mounting resignation and embitterment about the
Nazi regime. Spengler was ignored by official Nazi
Germany until his death in 1936, and he was only
reluctantly acknowledged by Alfred Rosenberg, the
party's ideologist. Although he had helped to smooth
the way for Hitler before 1933, Spengler was too
intelligent and aristocratic not to be repelled by the
hysteria and by the swaggering lack of moderation
in Hitler's character. He had the sagacity to realize
the pathological radicalism and the inner void of
Nazism.

Spengler remarked with prophetic sarcasm, in a
letter written in the spring of 1936, that "in ten years
the German Reich would probably no longer exist."[2]
Spengler's belated contempt for National Socialism
was prompted by his search behind the façade and
his insight into the real nature of the Third Reich. As
an unknown quantity before 1933, National Socialism
attracted the most divergent hopes and aspirations,
but now it had become a concrete, unavoidable reality.
Spengler's public silence after 1933 represents the
confession of his great error. His vision of the future
had served the Nazis as a convenient philosophic and
historical decoration.

Spengler is only one link in a chain which winds
through all the years of Nazism. It is the history of
disappointed longings, of increasing withdrawal from
Nazism or opposition to it, of resignation, and the
expulsion of people who originally belonged to the
NSDAP or who were close to Nazism or who had their
hopes pinned on it and helped to smooth the path for
it. Comparable to the belated disappointment of Oswald
Spengler is that of August Winnig, who in 1933 still
saw in the Nazi revolution "the great return" of the
German people to itself, and the victory of high values
over materialism. Winnig turned away more and more
from Hitler and eventually found his way into the
circles of the resistance movement. Another of the
disillusioned was Edgar J. Jung, who was murdered

[2]*Hans Frank*. Im Angesicht des Galgens *(Facing the Gallows)*,
Munich-Gräfelfing, 1953, p. 255. *Hans Frank had once been
strongly influenced by Spengler.*

in the purge of 30 June 1934. His book *Die Herrschaft der Minderwertigen* (The Rule of the Inferior), which appeared in 1927, coined one of the most effective metaphors in the fight against the Weimar Republic. Not even Moeller van den Bruck escaped Rosenberg's censorship during the Nazi era. He had been the idol of the young conservative revolutionaries and, with his major work *Das Dritte Reich* (The Third Reich), had helped as early as 1923—two years before his death—to prepare the minds for Hitler. Persons such as Friedrich Hielscher, Max Habermann, the Jünger brothers, Hermann Ullmann, and many others belonged, prior to 1933, to the most effective group of intellectual prophets of the revolutionary movement. They wanted the total rejuvenation of the state along chauvinistic lines. The use these men made of their journalistic talents, often in a radically aggressive fashion, and the esteem in which they were generally held lent significance to their work, directed toward bringing about a future of which they themselves had only hazy notions. Their influence defamed the parliamentary system and its liberal-humanitarian foundations. Faced with the realities of the Third Reich, these persons joined the ranks of the common *Fronde,* or resistance element, which began to crystallize regardless of earlier political identifications. As a protest, it was based on the elementary feeling for right and decency, against Hitler's barbaric inhumanity and his irresponsible policy which consistently courted catastrophe.

Characteristic of the extent of the German crisis

of conscience which preceded the coming of the Third
Reich is the fact that for some time many German
academicians and university teachers, as well as a
number of representatives of the artistic elite of
Germany were identified with Nazism. They announced
the need for a new start, prophesied a striking
historical turning point and a new era which would
replace the unpleasant political and social conditions
between 1918 and 1933. For a time these persons
embraced Nazism. Even the poet Gottfried Benn,
whose sublime feelings should have enabled him to
see through the masquerade of National Socialism,
defended the Nazi state in 1933, and lent himself to
a polemic against the German poets and writers who
had emigrated. In an open letter, written in the spring
of 1933, he called them sarcastically "troubadours
of progress" and "amateurs of civilization." He told
them that they should finally realize that the significance of the Third Reich was not in its form of
government, but that it represented "a new vision of
the birth of mankind, perhaps the last grand concept
of the white race, probably one of the greatest
realizations of the world spirit."[3] Years later the
same Gottfried Benn wrote in his diary, with resigned,
sarcastic perplexity:

"Who among us is not constantly occupied with
the one question—how was it possible and is it

[3]*Gottfried Benn.* Der neue Staat und die Intellektuellen *(The
New State and the Intellectuals),* Stuttgart/Berlin, *1933, p. 27.*

still possible today that Germany loyally followed
this so-called government, these half-dozen
brawlers, who have for ten years periodically
paraded the same nonsense in the same halls
before the same howling listeners—these six
jokers, who believe that they alone know everything better than the centuries before them and
the intelligence of the rest of the world?"[4]

The susceptibility to Nazism of the German bourgeoisie and of the intellectual elite, and the depth of
their intellectual corruption is an indication of the
fact that Hitler cannot simply be taken as a fatal
"accident" of German history, but must be regarded
as typical of special predispositions which go far
back into Teutonic intellectual history. On the other
hand, the examples mentioned show that the most
important instances of intellectual support for Hitler
were only temporary, and that they were based on a
cardinal misinterpretation. Hardly any facet of power
in German history prior to the Nazi movement relied
to such a degree intellectually, morally, and politically
on the support and on the devotion of those who did
not even belong to it—or misunderstood it basically
and mistook it for their own inarticulate fantasies
and longings. In all probability, such a blind intellectual subjectivity, rather than Nazi propaganda, helped
for many years to hide the reality of Nazism.
    Nazism deceived not only its broad following, but

[4]*Gottfried Benn.* Provoziertes Leben *(Life Challenged), Berlin, 1956, p. 159ff.*

the insiders as well. The history of the NSDAP itself is full of dissonances and contradictions, which centered on the question of the aim and nature of National Socialism. The discord over "true" Nazism started within the NSDAP itself. This became evident well before 1923. In the Munich section (*Ortsgruppe*) of the NSDAP, for example, a number of resignations from the party took place. Accusations were directed against the demagogic, aggressive course which Hitler, after his entry into the party at the end of 1919, tried to force on the National Socialist Workers Association (*Nationalsozialistischer Arbeiterverein*) founded by Anton Drexler.

One of the earliest cases of overt opposition occurred on 14 July 1921, when Hitler presented an ultimatum in which he demanded the party leadership and additional authority for himself. A group of old members of the NSDAP took a strong position against this demand in a bitter pamphlet and attempted to protect the "true" National Socialism from Hitler. In their proclamation to the Munich membership of the NSDAP they said, among other things:

> "National Socialists!
> "Don't be deceived. Hitler is a demagogue who relies on his gift of oratory. He believes that he can mislead the German people and talk you into believing things which are anything but the truth. Protest against this attempt to violate the honest foundation of the NSDAP, as has happened to other parties, which were misdirected through megalomania and demagogues! Show that there

is still a true German party which has the
courage to admit its mistakes and to remove
enemies which it mistook for honest people! Only
in this way will the party succeed to reawaken
the confidence of the German people which has
been lost on account of such Hitler-type charac-
ters."[5]

The seemingly paradoxical criticism of Hitler by
"honest" National Socialists reveals the heterogeneity
of the National Socialist movement. Until 1933 and
later it united many diverse powers and political
directions. In the course of the development of the
NSDAP, the "old fighters," especially those who had
played a leading role in the beginning as ideologists
of the party, formed an opposition or withdrew. Gottfried Feder, Alfred Rosenberg, and Hans Frank are
characteristic examples.

During the early Munich years of the National
Socialist movement, the insecure NSDAP was still
looking for catchy phrases with which to express its
rather undigested *völkisch* and nationalist ideas in a
poignant manner. A man like Gottfried Feder, a civil
engineer, with his world improvement idea of the
abolition of "interest slavery," could exert considerable influence as the party theorist and in developing
the program. Amateurish as his economic and political
thoughts were, at least he had a plan, which he
pursued with missionary zeal. Hitler had eagerly

[5]*A copy of this pamphlet is in the Bavarian Secret State
Archives.*

seized Feder's theory in 1919 and asserts in *Mein Kampf* that it had been a revelation to him of "immense importance for the future of the German people." However, it will be demonstrated that the type of ideologist like Feder, who honestly believed in his theories and who saw in the NSDAP a party which ought to be guided by these ideas and should be responsible for carrying them out, had no future in Hitler's party.

After a few years, Feder felt compelled to complain to Hitler that he and other nationalist veterans of the party were not consulted often enough by Hitler. A letter to Hitler of 10 August 1923 is the curious testimony of a man who confuses his concept of National Socialism with the NSDAP transformed by Hitler. Feder wrote:

"...We gladly grant you the honor to be the first, although only the first among otherwise free and equal men, as it has been the old Germanic tradition. We miss in you the need for close contact with your collaborators and the men who work in the same direction....We gladly give you the first place, but we have no sympathy for tyrannical inclinations..."[6]

With increasing disappointment over Hitler's opportunism, his faithlessness toward the original National Socialist idea, Feder drifted into the ideo-

---

[6]*Complete text of Feder's letter in Oron James Hale, ed.,* Journal of Modern History, *1958, XXX, pp. 358-362.*

logical opposition to Hitler which formed within the party. Although he submitted to him time and again, as late as December 1932, he and Gregor Strasser had already decided to leave the party. Feder's influence continued to diminish, especially since Hitler courted the bourgeoisie, industry, and representatives of the banks to an ever increasing degree after his alliance with Alfred Hugenberg and the election triumph of 1930. With sure instinct for propagandistic expediency, Hitler realized that association of the NSDAP with men like Feder would seem ridiculous to the bourgeois economists. Hans Reupke, one of the economic experts who had joined the Nazis, declared in 1931: the original "much too mechanistic" anticapitalist slogan of National Socialism has today been improved "to an antimaterialistic one." One needed no longer "concern oneself seriously with the demand for the abolition of interest slavery" in the extreme form in which it had originally emerged.[7]

After Hugenberg left Hitler's cabinet in June 1933, Feder was given as consolation prize the post of an undersecretary under the Nazi Minister of Economics Karl Schmitt. When Hjalmar Schacht took over the Ministry of Economics from Schmitt, in December 1934, one of his first steps was to dismiss Feder. No one spoke up for him. For another year the discredited party ideologist functioned fairly well as a Commissioner for Land Settlement. Then he was granted a professorship at the Technical University

[7]*Hans Reupke.* Der Nationalsozialismus und die Wirtschaft *(National Socialism and the Economy), Berlin, 1931, p. 30.*

in Berlin. When Feder died on 24 September 1941, the
Nazi press took hardly any notice of his passing. The
official Nazi newspaper *Völkischer Beobachter* limited
itself to a small obituary notice on 26 September 1941.

Alfred Rosenberg, the main ideologist of National
Socialism deserves mention, as a parallel to the
Gottfried Feder case. During the Nazi struggle for
power Rosenberg had good reason to count himself
among the leading figures of Hitler's meager brain-
trust. He exercised considerable influence during
this period as editor of the *Völkischer Beobachter,*
and as Hitler's advisor on foreign affairs. His growing
estrangement from Hitler began with the increase in
power of the NSDAP. One of Rosenberg's first great
disappointments came from the fact that Hitler
refused to proclaim Rosenberg's *Mythus des 20 Jahrhunderts* (Myth of the 20th Century), published in 1930,
as the official and binding dogma for the NSDAP. Rosenberg was later forced to acknowledge his "Bible of
National Socialism" as only his personal ideology.
Rosenberg's influence in the party hierarchy declined
rapidly after 1933. His position as *Reichsleiter*
of the NSDAP and the accumulation of his official
positions—head of the Foreign Office of the NSDAP,
Plenipotentiary for the Supervision of Intellectual and
Ideological Education, Minister for the Occupied
Eastern Territories—cannot conceal the fact that he
no longer played a decisive role in any of the impor-
tant departments of the Third Reich. During World
War II he had already been eliminated from the circle
of Hitler's most important advisors. In foreign affairs,
Joachim von Ribbentrop, whom he hated, had gained

the upper hand. In cultural affairs Joseph Goebbels proved a superior rival. The party Gauleiter appointed as Commissioners in the occupied eastern territories, and Heinrich Himmler's officials rode roughshod over Rosenberg's subtle political concepts with their brutal master race policy. Rosenberg fell into a tragicomic role. He was caught in jurisdictional struggles, and in trouble with almost all the mighty of the Third Reich. He was deeply disappointed by Hitler. Rosenberg saw himself as the last guardian of the "true" National Socialism and of its ideology, whose original purity had been long betrayed by the power-mad Gauleiter—the provincial party chiefs— and the party satraps in Hitler's immediate circle. The published fragments of Rosenberg's diary notes of this time testify to this "inner alienation" of the party's theorist which borders on the grotesque.[8]

A further example of this confused opposition to Hitler in the name of the ideology of National Socialism is provided by the career of Hans Frank and his attitude on judicial developments in the Third Reich. Point 19 of the party program of 1920 contained the demand for a "new German Community law" instead of those parts of the Roman law which were determined by individualism and thus not practical in the government of a people living in a closely associated community(*Völkisches Gemeinschaftsleben*).The

---

[8]Das politische Tagebuch Alfred Rosenbergs *(Alfred Rosenberg's Political Diary)*, edited by *Hans-Günther Seraphim, Göttingen/Berlin/Frankfurt, 1956.*

traditional liberal laws were to be modernized and replaced by *völkisch* laws, based on old Germanic examples. A so-called living people's law, stemming from the intuition of the people, was to take the place of positive law, and of the logical interpretation of learned jurisprudence.

The young Munich lawyer Dr. Hans Frank was among Hitler's closest collaborators during the 1920's, and he was the most vocal supporter of such a National Socialist folk jurisprudence. As Hitler's defense attorney, and that of the NSDAP in numerous trials, Frank rapidly became the acknowledged "crown jurist" of the party. He could therefore hope to become Minister of Justice in case the NSDAP seized control of the government, and would thereby have the opportunity to realize his concepts of legal reform. Instead, no massive revision of the content of the existing laws took place after 1933. As in the case of Feder's theses, it appeared that the nebulous Nazi theories about the revision of the laws, e.g. concepts like the "correct popular instinct" were not practical because of their ambiguity. Therefore what developed in the Third Reich was not a revolutionary, unified "new law," but an opportunistic combination of elements of the old constitutional state and the new lawless police state. Hitler showed he was primarily interested in the removal of those constitutional and judicial principles which were a limitation on his exercise of power. He was not concerned with the codification of a new Nazi law which would have been binding on himself as well as on the party and on Himmler's SS and police. Hitler preferred, therefore,

to co-operate with Franz Gürtner, the Minister of
Justice, a member of the German Nationalist Party.
Hitler had inherited Gürtner from the von Papen
cabinet in 1933, and kept him until his death in 1941.
He preferred him to Hans Frank, who as one of the
old guard would have been somewhat harder to control.
As head of the *Reichsrechtsamt,* the Judicial Department of the NSDAP, as president of the Academy for
German Law, and as head of the *NS-Rechtswahrer-
bundes,* the Nazi League for the Legal Profession,
Frank retained sufficient opportunities to speak out
on his ideas for a German *völkisch* reform of the law.
With the backing of the party press he was able for
many years to intimidate the Ministry of Justice
whenever it did not show the required measure of
justice ''close to the people.'' However, Frank remained excluded from the administration and minis-
terial direction of justice. As an illustration of the
course of events one can cite the fate of the projected
revision of criminal law during the early years of
the Third Reich. With the collaboration of Frank and
Roland Freisler, a new criminal code had been
developed by a Criminal Law Commission during
the years 1933-1936. It was to base the whole criminal
law on *völkisch* principles. When it came to approving
the completed draft, Hitler, supported by Goebbels
and Himmler, again and again avoided doing so. The
new Nazi criminal law code, announced by Frank with
great fanfare, never saw the light of day. Here,
as with other matters, it became apparent that
Hitler disdained established laws, and wanted them
removed to avoid restrictions in his own actions.

He opposed the principle of legality itself.

Even before the outbreak of the war in 1939, the position of Frank in the party became noticeably weaker. Instead of Frank's Judicial Department of the NSDAP, which was dissolved in 1942, the Judicial Department of the Party Chancellery under Martin Bormann finally developed into the controlling arm of the party; on its decisions the legislative work of all ministries had depended from 1941/1942. Frank, who had been one of the most eager admirers of Hitler and who had worked for years on the embellishment of the absolutism of the Führer, by announcing that law and the will of the Führer were identical, was set aside. He still had some residual faith in the ideology and did not realize that the hybrid construction of a "National Socialist state of justice," for which he searched, was neither a state of law in the old sense nor a police state, but a hopeless dream.

As Governor General of Poland, Frank had the supreme responsibility for the unimaginable acts of violence and exterminations which were carried out by Himmler's SS and police commandos. Yet, after three years, in 1942, he took a public stand against the development of the Third Reich into a terroristic police state. In a series of lectures he defended the eternal nature of law, without which no community could exist. Frank's defense was directed against the steadily increasing arbitrary tyranny of the SS and the party.[9] This protest, which differenti-

[9]*Excerpts from these lectures in Hans Frank,* Im Angesicht des Galgens, *p. 464ff.*

ates the otherwise very unstable Hans Frank in a favorable human manner from such types as Reinhard Heydrich and Martin Bormann, cost him all his judicial offices in the NSDAP in August 1942. He was also forbidden to make speeches, and it was probably because of a last, forgiving sentiment of loyalty on Hitler's part that Frank was merely degraded to being a persona non grata in the party, but was allowed to retain his position as Governor General in Poland.

Frank's sanguine protest against the police state terrorism of the Third Reich could hardly qualify as an act of intellectual opposition. It was further weakened by the fact that Frank maintained his loyalty to Hitler until 1945. Frank did not understand that one could not fight the reality of Nazism with an imaginary National Socialist ideology. He became the Don Quixote of the Nazi movement.

3. Nationalist Ideology and the National Socialist Movement

The examples presented so far give an insight into the struggle of persons and powers within the immediate and more remote circles of the NSDAP. All of them claimed to represent the "true" National Socialism. These claims only added to the confusing medley of appearance and reality of Nazism. The movement was a riddle to its contemporaries, and it is still difficult for a historian to unravel fact from fancy. This makes it even more urgent to pursue the question concerning the ideology of Nazism and its significance to the development and reality of the NSDAP.

The ideology and the practical political program of
the NSDAP was from the very beginning not the
result of an original, self-sufficient analysis of the
present, or a rational proposal of a system for the future. Nazism was never an idea in the sense of intellectual penetration of political, national, social, or even
biological conditions. The chain of ideological dissonances and disappointments which marked the
party's path from the outset, are only the reflection
of these basic logical disagreements in this so-called
Nazi interpretation of life. As an ideology, Nazism is
therefore basically different from Marxism with its
inner logic. The vague, the accidental, and the
conscious discrepancy from the time of the establishment of the NSDAP, belong to the characteristic of
its presumed ideas. One could rightfully speak of
Nazi ideology as a catch-all, a conglomeration, a
hodgepodge of ideas. To approach Nazi ideology with
the usual measuring devices of intellectual history is
therefore possible only with the greatest reservation.
One certainly has to refer to Herder, Fichte, Hegel,
Arndt, Jahn, and others, if one wishes to grasp the
elements of the nationalistic, ideological environment,
which provided such exceptionally favorable conditions
for the growth of Nazism in Germany. However, it
would be a mistake to speak of an individually trace-
able direction or of an intellectual, ideological school
in accordance with the classical thought pattern of
intellectual history. Alone, the manipulations which
were necessary during the Third Reich to make
ideological and propagandistic use of some apparent

intellectual precursors should prevent linking Nazism too directly to Germany's past. Rosenberg's strained interpretation of Meister Eckehart and Alfred Bäumler's book on Nietzsche are examples. Insofar as one can speak at all of a genesis of the Nazi conglomeration of ideas, it is less understandable from any one intellectual influence than from the conceptions, examples, sentiments, and resentments which began to form the taste of the masses and the intellectual world of the German nationalist bourgeoisie since the second half of the 19th century. The disjointed self-assurance of a bourgeoisie that unexpectedly was propelled into national power and rapid prosperity, laid the groundwork for these influences through an inner awareness of its own kind and its superiority. The philosophies of Fichte, Hegel, or Nietzsche did not contribute as much to Germany's pre-Hitlerian intellectual background for National Socialism as commemorations of the victory at Sedan (in the Franco-Prussian War), Bismarckian blood-and-iron quotations, the historical novels of Felix Dahn, and mass editions of sentimental "house and homeland" poets. The bourgeoisie mistook the arrogant nationalism and race teachings of Paul Lagarde, Julius Langbehn, Count Gobineau, Karl Dühring, and Houston Stewart Chamberlain for knowledge of the world.

The political situation which became more critical during the First World War and the immediate postwar period, almost in one stroke aroused the doctrine of a German mission and unique German character which up to that time had been latent as a

"harmless" bourgeois-patriotic conviction. This becomes clear by the number of anti-Semitic organizations, *völkisch* clubs, party groups, and associations
which were formed from isolated prewar roots in
Germany after 1918 and began to sprout with abandon.
These joined the great nationalist patriotic organizations from the Wilhelmian period, such as the
Ostmarkenverein (Eastern Provinces Association),
the *Wehrverein* (Military Association), and the *Alldeutscher Verband* (Pan-German League), and the
smaller anti-Semitic nationalist prewar organizations
and circles, such as Friedrich Lange's *Deutschbund*
(German League), Theodor Fritsch's *Reichshammer-
bund* (Reich Hammer League), and many others. The
Pan-German League had grown to 490 local groups
by 1920 and had officially adopted anti-Semitism into
its program, in the *Bamberger Erklärung* of 1919. In
the year 1918 the *Deutschvölkischer Schutz- und
Trutzbund* (German *Völkisch* Protection and Defense
League) was established under its eager business manager Alfred Roth; it reached 30,000 members within two
years. In 1920 the *Hochschulring deutscher Art*
(University Circle of German Character) was formed
as the collective association of German nationalist
movements at the universities. In the same year the
Vereinigung Völkischer Verleger (Alliance of *Völkisch*
Publishers), and its monthly journal *Deutsches
Schrifttum* (German Writings) edited by Professor
Adolf Bartels, made its appearance under the leadership of Dr. Kellermann of the Alexander Duncker
publishing house. In addition to these, there were
organizations like the *Vaterländischer Volksbund*

(People's Fatherland League), 1918; the *Treubund deutscher Dichter, Musiker und Künstler* (Fidelity League of German Poets, Musicians, and Artists), 1920; the *Jungborn Bund* (Fountain of Youth League), 1918; the *Gesellschaft deutsch-germanischer Gesittung* (Association for German-Nordic Morality), 1915; . the *Germanischer Gewissensbund* (League for Germanic Conscience), 1920; the *Deutsch-völkischer Studentenverband* (German *Völkisch* Student Association), 1920; the *Bund für deutsche Erneuerung* (League for German Regeneration), and many more.

A list of "German *völkisch* unions, societies, federations, and orders," which Alfred Roth published in 1921, counted no less than 73 organized *völkisch* groups of which most were founded only after the end of the First World War. Even if the majority of these were unimportant, together they give a clear picture of the extent and infection of the feverish atmosphere of that exalted nationalist extremism which permeated Germany ever since 1918/1919. This extremism also expressed itself in the contemporary literature of these years. The ideological ignorance of these groups and their literature—in which race mysticism and pseudo-biology were mixed with Nordic-German historical legend, creation of neopagan religions, promotion of nationalist art pursuits and agrarian ideologies, all coupled with anti-Semitic intolerance—characterized the pan-German nationalist activity. These were the historical roots of the NSDAP and its ideology. The early Nazis emerged from the Thule Society and other groups. The Munich Thule Society was the local group of the

German *Völkisch* Protection and Defense League, and
it included Rosenberg, Feder and Frank among its
adherents. It found in the Munich of the era after the
Bavarian Soviet Republic (1919) a fertile field for
agitation. The early Nazis also came from the
splinter parties such as the *völkisch* German-Social
Party, which followed the tradition of the Anti-
Semite's Party which preceded it during the Empire.
From it Julius Streicher and his vituperative newspaper *Stürmer* (Attacker) emerged. One of these
early Nazis was the *völkisch* poet Dietrich Eckart,
who purchased the *Völkischer Beobachter* for the
NSDAP in 1920.

The development in Stuttgart is another example:
shortly before the turn of the century a small group
of Young Germans was formed under the influence
of the local activity of the anti-Semitic Reform Party
of the 1890's. These individuals were greatly impressed by the writings of Lagarde, Adolf Stöcker,
Karl Dühring, Otto Glagau, the translations of
Gobineau by Ludwig Schemann, the *Antisemitenkate-
chismus* (Catechism for anti-Semites) by Theodor
Fritsch, and the *Germanenbücher* (Germanic Books)
by Ludwig Wilser, Ludwig Woltmann, and Gustaf Kos-
sinnas. In 1906 the group joined with Theodor Fritsch's
Stuttgart *Hammer-Gesellschaft* (Hammer Association)
which had been established about 1900, to form a circle
of about a hundred members under the leadership
of Richard Haug. The combined organization was
closely connected with the *Alldeutscher Verband*
(Pan-German League). During 1918/1919 the mem-

bership multiplied rapidly and merged into the local chapter of the German *Völkisch* Protection and Defense League, which had been founded in the meantime. On 7 May 1920 it held a spectacular meeting at the Dinkelacker Hall in Stuttgart. Hitler had been invited as the speaker. This gathering led to the formation of the Stuttgart cell of the NSDAP from persons who had been members of the Protection and Defense League.[10] There can be no doubt that the anti-Semitic, *völkisch*, all-German sects constituted the organizational as well as ideological and historical starting point of Nazism.

Recently we received interesting and well-documented proof that Hitler obtained the specific imprint of his anti-Semitic ideas, regarding the poisoning of the world by Jewry as expressed in *Mein Kampf*, from his early days in Vienna.[11] One can note repeatedly in his stereotyped remarks regarding the "Jewish question," that Hitler received his youthful impressions from one of the most occult sources which flourished in the Austrian capital in those days. These were the journalistic aberrations of a religious

---

[10]*Hauptarchiv der NSDAP, photocopies in the Institut für Zeitgeschichte, Munich, the National Archives, Washington, and the Hoover Institution, Stanford; (hereafter cited as HA/NSDAP), Fa 88, Fasc. 166.*

[11]*Wilfried Daim.* Der Mann, der Hitler die Ideen gab. Von den religiösen Verirrungen eines Sektierers zum Rassenwahn eines Diktators *(The Man Responsible for Hitler's Ideas. From the Religious Aberrations of a Sectarian to the Race Mania of a Dictator), Munich, 1958.*

sectarian who developed his so-called "theo-zoology" under the assumed name of Jörg Lanz von Liebenfels. Liebenfels' distortions recast the Biblical revelations and the whole history of mankind into the race mythology of a primeval battle between the blond god-man, the Aryan hero, and his opposite, the racially base animal-man.

One hardly needs this specific documentation to show the intellectual chaos, the frightening lack of foundation, and the moral perversion which characterizes the Nazi ideological literature. Rosenberg's *Mythus*, Walter Darre's "mystique of blood and soil", the writings of the race theoretician Hans F. K. Günther (who was appointed professor at the University of Jena in 1931 by Wilhelm Frick in spite of faculty opposition), and similar Nazi literature speak for themselves. Hermann Rauschning, the disillusioned Nazi who knew the intellectual calibre of Nazism from personal experience, summarized his judgment in the following words: "No enemy could demand greater degradation of the German nation than to accept and to believe this ideology."[12] To those who kept their intellectual independence from this ideological activity, or what passed as this among Nazis and their adherents, elevation of this ideology to a state doctrine in 1933 must have appeared as a mummery unique in world history. Karl Kraus described it as incantations of

---

[12]*Hermann Rauschning*. Die Revolution des Nihilismus. Kulisse und Wirklichkeit im 3. Reich *(The Revolution of Nihilism. Staging and Reality in the Third Reich)*, *Zurich, 1938, p. 84.*

witches at the Walpurgis Night.[13]

The history of these years becomes intelligible only if one considers the situation at the time. Although much of the hero-worshipping race mystique—the core of Nazism—was rejected during the Weimar period as a bastard religion by critical contemporaries, many moods found expression in it which were much more significant than an expression of sects or the *völkisch* orders, Germanic federations, and Nordic regeneration societies. Such political myths and emotional values were legion, years before Hitler's appearance on the scene. The dynamic nationalism born out of the disappointments of the First World War and the Treaty of Versailles helped to magnify the appeal of a warped ideology: the passionate antiliberalism, in part connected with what Gregor Strasser called the "anticapitalistic longing"; the avoidance of political realities by creating a dream world of folk idylls, or by retreat into the heroism of the Germanic and medieval period; the transformation of the experiences of the First World War into a rebirth of the German people; the radical negation of the humanistic educational tradition of the Enlightenment and of civilization; and the esthetic worship of leadership, power, and primeval origins. These and many other strange ideas were taken over, especially by Germany's intellectual elite, and passed on to the Nazis, decorated with fancy literary trimmings. The

---

[13]*Karl Kraus.* Die dritte Walpurgisnacht *(The Third Witches' Sabbath), Munich, 1952.*

breakdown of the traditional bourgeois order was a
result of the war, postwar, and inflation period. The
fragmentation of bourgeois political and sociological
patterns became evident with the Freikorps and
other paramilitary organizations. Hitler's Storm
Troopers (SA) and Black Guard (SS) were patterned
after these. Aside from the foreign and domestic
crises, this breakdown was the real cause for the
internal crisis of conscience and the universal development of the activist-revolutionary tendencies of
pronounced anti-intellectual and anti-civilization attitudes. These attitudes were colored by the glorified
prophecy presenting irrational pictures of the future,
the revelation of ideas about a new order and the
negation of the parliamentary Weimar Republic, and
those who represented it. In these ideas lay the real
intellectual seduction which emanated from Oswald
Spengler, from Moeller van den Bruck and others
who wrote during the Weimar period. These ideas
contributed greatly to the weakening of the German
bourgeois academicians' intellectual resistance to
the monstrous Nazi ideology. Even long after 1933
numerous respected intellectuals, writers, and pub-
licists mistook Hitler for their noble German ideal.
With a strange self-deception they celebrated in him
the coming of a second Luther and enjoyed making
other historical parallels. They gave to Hitler that
charismatic nimbus which he needed and which
provided for the NSDAP the façade which it lacked
to hide its own intellectual and ideological insig-
nificance.

Thomas Mann, who immediately after his emigration in 1933 became aware of these academic hymns of praise which were sung after Hitler took power, wrote bitterly in his diary:

"The primitiveness, the disappearance of culture, the increase in stupidity and the reduction to a petit bourgeois mentality are not recognized as fright by the intellectuals but are welcomed with a perverted approval. Propagators of the irrational, as they prevailed in great masses in Germany during the period of growing National Socialism, educated the people to a moral sans-culottism and to an apathy to all cruelty....

Cryptic sciences, pseudosciences and frauds, formation of sects and quackery were the vogue and had a mass appeal. Intellectuals did not consider all this as a low, modern fad, or as a cultural degradation. Instead they welcomed it as the rebirth of mystic powers of life and of the soul of the people. The soil was ready for the most absurd and lowest political mass superstition. That was the faith in Adolf Hitler."[14]

However, the faith of many circles of the intelligentsia and the German bourgeoisie in Adolf Hitler, of which Thomas Mann wrote, was not simply identical with the faith in the *völkisch* anti-Semitic ideology

[14]*Thomas Mann*. Leiden an Deutschland. Tagebuchblätter aus dem Jahre 1933/34. Im Bd. "Zeit und Werk" (*Suffering for Germany. Diary Pages from the Year 1933/34, in the volume "Time and Works"*), Berlin, 1956, p. 105ff.

of Nazism. This was often unwillingly accepted in the
bargain when a German declared himself to favor
Hitler. The beginnings of the NSDAP which show the
ideological origins of the Nazi movement should not
hide the fact that its specific appeal, the successes
of Hitler with the German public, did not stem from
ideological sources alone. During the decisive years
of the party's rise (1929-1932), the suggestive powers
of the Hitler movement rested less on the similarities
with other *völkisch* anti-Semitic groups than on some
additional appeals of the Nazi movement. It is necessary to show how the Nazis went beyond the thinking
and practices of the *völkisch*.

Ideologically, there was little difference in the
early years between the *völkisch* groups and the
NSDAP. The ideological part of Nazism fitted easily
into the *völkisch* concept. Differences of emphasis
existed among the *völkisch* groups. Some were
primarily concerned with a reawakening of Germanic
and Nordic values and attitudes toward life, while
others were first and foremost concerned with a so-
called folk culture or a *völkisch* economic and state
order. Still others were aggressively jingoistic Protestants who saw in the fight against Rome the focal
point of a German *völkisch* rebirth, or individuals who
found the same device useful exclusively in the re-
pression of the Jews. All of these nuances were represented in the NSDAP, as well as in the rest of the
völkisch groups. There was no basic ideological difference among them. These elements were contained
in the Austrian Pan-German movement *(Schönerer-
Bewegung)* before the First World War, as well as

among the German anti-Semitic groups of the Imperial period. Völkisch and Nazi ideology were identical, if one understands by ideology a composite of intellectual attitudes. Hitler expressed this when he wrote in Mein Kampf: "The basic ideas of the National Socialist movement are völkisch, and the völkisch ideas are National Socialist."

Nevertheless, from the outset of his political career as a demagogic propagandist and finally as chairman of the NSDAP (from 29 July 1921 on), Hitler never ceased in his efforts to change the image of a völkisch club, which the NSDAP presented in its early years with its political discussion circles. Hitler instinctively recognized the decisive weakness of most of the völkisch circles and party clubs: their ideological and organizational sectarianism and their bourgeois-philistine basis and vocabulary could not be disguised by their aggressive ideology. In a memorandum of the year 1922, entitled Der völkische Gedanke und die Partei (The völkisch idea and the party), Hitler wrote that the German völkisch movement is sterile and powerless because of "its total lack of understanding of the fact that an idea is of no value, as long as the wish does not turn into action, but eternally remains a wish."[15] It is necessary, instead, "to change this idea into political power" and to create an "organization of power." In numerous places in Mein Kampf, Hitler repeated this formula more pointedly and in diverse forms, and talked with cynical irony about the "old fashioned völkisch

[15]HA/NSDAP, Fa 88, Fasc. 46.

theoreticians." He belittled those "German *völkisch*
wandering scholars whose positive contribution always
equals zero," those "who dream of Old-Germanic
heroism, of the dim past, of stone axes, spear and
shield, but who in reality are the biggest cowards,"
and whose "miserable hypocrisy" seems merely
comic to the general public. Hitler had to free the
NSDAP from its belief in "intellectual weapons" and
"quiet work" as a means to accomplish the nationalist
regeneration. "Any ideology, even though a thousand
times correct and of the greatest value for humanity,
remains without importance as long as its basic
concepts have not become the banner of a fighting
movement....A political program must be formed
from general concepts and a specific political belief
from a general ideology." The creation of a "limited,
tightly organized political faith and fighting association, unified intellectually and in purpose," is the
"most important accomplishment, because on it
depends the hope for the victory of the idea."

He also declared in *Mein Kampf*: "The incorporation
of the *völkisch* ideology into a party" in the form of
the NSDAP is the only way to victory. "An ideology
can fight and win not in the unlimited freedom of
interpretation of a general idea, but instead in the
limited form of a political organization." The "attempt
to represent the *völkisch* idea outside the NSDAP" is
impossible and "when anyone accuses the movement
of acting as if it had borrowed the *völkisch* idea"
there was "only one answer to this: *Not only has it
been borrowed, but it was created specifically for
this practical use.*" Despite temporary tactical al-

liances, combination of voting lists of candidates during elections, and similar joint efforts, into which Hitler entered with individual *völkisch* parties or groups until 1927-1928, he was never interested in the *völkisch* movement as such, but only in the NSDAP. He continued to hold fast to its right to an exclusive rule.

After his release from a nine-months incarceration at the fortress of Landsberg on 20 December 1924, Hitler's primary effort consisted in disrupting the German *völkisch* front of the *Nationalsozialistische Freiheitsbewegung* (National Socialist Freedom Movement), which during the period of the prohibition of the NSDAP had been formed by Nazis and *völkisch* groups under the leadership of Albrecht von Graefe, General Erich von Ludendorff, and Gregor Strasser. This movement had received almost two million votes in the Reichstag elections of 4 May 1924. This success gave it thirty-two seats in the Reichstag, the lower house of the German parliament. Hitler refounded the NSDAP on 27 February 1925 under his direction, and strengthened the *Führerprinzip* (leadership principle) within the party. Primarily at Hitler's instigation no permanent coalition was developed between the followers of Ludendorff and those of the North German *Deutschvölkische Freiheitspartei* (German *Völkisch* Freedom Party) of Graefe and Reinhold Wulle, and other *völkisch* groups after 1925. Even the Stormtroopers (SA), which had been closely tied to other so-called patriotic vigilante associations and fighting leagues, were converted by Hitler into a pure arm of the NSDAP, although independent strains

continued to exist in the SA, until Hitler eradicated
these violently in the purge of 30 June 1934.

In *Mein Kampf*, Hitler had formulated the axiom:
"The *völkisch* state will never be created by a desire
for compromise by *völkisch* co-operation, but only
through the iron will of a single movement which has
succeeded against all." Not by merger, but only by
unconditional incorporation into the NSDAP could a
common front be formed.

Hitler ignored the fact that the NSDAP owed almost
everything to the *völkisch,* pan-German, anti-Semitic
organizations, during the first years of its existence.
He shunned no means to checkmate these organizations,
and to catch their votes for the NSDAP. For example:
the *völkisch* fighting organizations were particularly
strong in the state of Thuringia—such as the *Werwolf,
Reichskriegsflagge* (Imperial War Flag), and others.
They gave the NSDAP considerable aid during the
elections for the Thuringian state assembly *(Landtag)*
on 30 January 1927, by combining with them for
election propaganda and for a common list of candidates. But a few days later Hitler did not hesitate
to instruct his provincial party chief, Dr. Arthur
Dinter, to inform the Thuringian party comrades
that they could not hold dual membership in the
völkisch fighting organizations in the future, on
penalty of expulsion from the Nazi party. The representative of the Thuringian *völkisch* "Leader Circle,"
Count Görz, protested. Hitler replied on 23 February
1927 that the order to Dinter was only common sense.
Membership in two organizations was an absurdity.
"It is a mistake to count on a man who still belongs

to another organization, since one never knows whose orders he will follow in the end."[16]

The *völkisch* groups which repeatedly emphasized their willingness to work with the NSDAP and which complained about Hitler's "regrettable conviction of the necessity for an independently organized NSDAP,"[17] considered Hitler as a disrupting force, the "splinterer" of the *völkisch* movement, the traitor to their common beliefs, and the saboteur of urgently needed unity among those in the *völkisch* camp. The exclusive loyalty to the NSDAP demanded by Hitler, who considered it the only organization which was suited to bring about a consolidation of the *völkisch* movement, was not the only bone of contention. Cases increased in which Hitler gave up so-called "absolute" axioms of the *völkisch* program for tactical party-political and propagandistic considerations. One such incident was the question of claiming South Tyrol, whose polemic, propagandistic exploitation Hitler had rejected in *Mein Kampf,* out of consideration for Mussolini and a future policy of a German-Italian alliance. Among the *völkisch* groups and in the whole camp of the German nationalists (the conservative *Deutschnationale Partei)*, this renunciation of what was a basic revisionist demand

---

[16]*HA/NSDAP, Fa 88, Fasc. 137.*

[17]*Letter by the leader of the German Nationalist Freedom Party, von Graefe, to Siegfried Kasche, 17 June 1925 (HA/ NSDAP, Fa 88, Fasc. 199).*

by the *völkisch* groups was branded as a despicable "Southern Locarno."[18] Even in his own party Hitler met considerable resistance. Gottfried Feder had been appointed as editor of the *NS-Schriftenreihe* (Nazi publications) in 1926. This included the official commentary on the Program of the NSDAP beginning in 1927. In the explanation to Point 1 of the Nazi Program, "Union of all Germans in a Greater Germany," Feder was as yet able to state: "We do not renounce a single German in the Sudetenland, in South Tyrol, or in Austria, the colony of the League of Nations." This version remained until the 4th edition (1928) of Feder's official party commentary. In the 5th edition, of 1929, no further mention of South Tyrol was made.

Hitler's alleged alliance to Rome and the clericals played a scarcely less important role in the *völkisch* polemics against the NSDAP. The followers of Ludendorff and a number of North German *völkisch* Protestants took exception to Hitler's temporary cessation of the anti-clerical propaganda of the NSDAP. Hitler thought this necessary in order to create a more sympathetic attitude among the adherents of the (Catholic) Bavarian People's Party, which ruled in Munich, and to regain permission from the Bavarian government of Heinrich Held to make speeches in public. Count Ernst von Reventlow

[18]*Translator's note: This was a reference to the Treaty of Locarno, in which the government of the Weimar Republic had agreed in 1925 to respect the existing western borders of Germany.*

wrote on 7 February 1925 in the *Reichswart* (Guardian
of the Reich) "A peace with Rome" made it "impossible for the *völkisch* groups who had contracted
it to carry on a real and useful fight for the *völkisch*
idea." The *völkisch* criticism against the "Roman-
ized" NSDAP, which was accused of being "in the
pay of Fascism," received new stimulus when Hitler
and the *Völkischer Beobachter* acknowledged the
Lateran Treaties, concluded between Mussolini and
the Vatican in 1929, as the accomplishment of states-
men. This was also the background for the break
between Hitler and his Gauleiter of Thuringia, Arthur
Dinter, the author of the sensational novel, *Die
Sünde wider das Blut* (The Sin Against the Blood).
Dinter did not submit to Hitler's tactics and for
that reason was expelled from the NSDAP in 1928.
Dinter saw Luther as the first German *völkisch*
personality in German history and, like Alfred
Rosenberg, preached the fight against Rome as well
as the fight against Jewry. He wrote at the end of
1928 in his sectarian journal *Das Geistchristentum*
(Ideological Christianity):

> "Now only blind, uncritical admirers of Hit-
> ler's or those...who do not want to know the
> truth, can still doubt that the Hitler party is a
> Jesuit party, which pursues the business of
> Rome under the *völkisch* banner."

Some narrow-minded fanatics among the *völkisch*
groups attempted at times to prove that Hitler was
not really an anti-Semite. Here they were terribly

mistaken, as history proved. But these fanatics claimed that he would sooner or later abandon the whole anti-Semitic program of the NSDAP, when it became necessary to catch votes.[19]

Though this view of Hitler and the NSDAP may seem grotesque, coming from people who mistook a perverted loyalty to the barbarity of their so-called *völkisch* ideology for idealism, it does reveal something important: the theory of the NSDAP is unthinkable without recognizing that it had its origins partially in obscure sources of chauvinist ideology. The original core of the party, consisting mainly of *völkisch* sectarians, lost influence as National Socialism developed. They were, however, given the toleration reserved for court jesters and could in some measure participate in the formation of the image of National Socialism until 1945. Neither Hitler nor a considerable number of his staunchest and his most active followers—Max Amman, Göring, Goebbels, Bormann, and others—felt themselves bound by a detailed *völkisch* dogma. Although Hitler's oratory was completely permeated by elements of *völkisch* ideology, he did not pay much attention to a clarification of ideological questions, nor did he give any special consideration to systematic thought. More or less consciously and instinctively, Hitler omitted drawing definite, dogmatic and logical consequences from Nazi slogans. For instance, he never bothered to resolve the dilemma between "national" and "supranational" which developed, perforce, from such

---

[19]*Friedrich Plümer.* Die Wahrheit über Hitler und seinen Kreis *(The Truth about Hitler and His Circle), Munich, 1925.*

incongruous ideas as folk, race, nation, and Reich. Hitler's reaction to attempts to systematize the so-called Nazi philosophy of life through a detailed exposition was one of cynical amusement.[20]

A few very simple basic concepts or fixed ideas found in Hitler's earliest fanatic utterances are the exceptions. They recur for twenty-five years as stereotypes in his speeches and his writings. One of these fixed theories is the biologic-materialistic concept of the survival of the strong, which Hitler saw as the law, and also as the primary reason for existence in the life of peoples and individuals. Another fixed theory in the area of politics is the geopolitically-colored concept of the necessity and the mission of the German *Bodenpolitik* (settlement policy) which gave the nation the right to the acquisition of large areas in the East. These concepts, more than his anti-Bolshevism, drove him in 1941 to the adventure of the Russian campaign. These fixed ideas of Hitler's hardened into firm articles of faith. Only his anti-Semitic mania was stronger and grew to the proportions of a negative religion. Whatever psychological interpretations of his life experiences may indicate, Hitler's hatred of the Jews made up the most constant factor in all his willful political life. It was the dominant aggressive drive, possibly the only one of his ideological "convictions" which was not open to opportunistic manipulation. While there

[20]*See H. Picker*, Hitlers Tischgespräche im Führerhauptquartier 1941-1942 *(Hitler's Table Talks)*, Bonn, 1951, p. 275. *Hitler remarked that he "like many Gauleiter" had only "read a small portion" of Rosenberg's Mythus des 20 Jahrhunderts.*

are crass discrepancies between the ideological
phraseology and the reality of Nazism almost everywhere else, in this matter the singlemindedness of the
possessed is evident. He was true to his idea and
carried his anti-Jewish hate propaganda to the extreme
of systematic, assembly line genocide. At the end of
1944, for example, Hitler and Himmler ordered
SS commandos, transport facilities, and diplomatic-
political initiatives to speed the transport of the
remaining one-third of the Hungarian Jews to the
gas chambers of Auschwitz. At that time Soviet
forces had already penetrated deeply into Hungary,
and military considerations should have argued against
such shipments of the Jews. This clearly shows that
the drive for it did not stem from rational motives,
but came out of deranged ideological attitudes. The
expression of satisfaction over the fate of millions
of murdered Jews and the exhortation to the German
people to maintain the race laws passed at the
Nuremberg Party Rally in 1935, therefore, logically
became the last word which Hitler had to say in
his testament, immediately before his suicide:

"Above all, I hold the leadership of the nation
and my followers responsible for the most
painstaking adherence to the racial laws and to
the most merciless opposition to the world-wide
poisoner of all peoples, international Jewry.
Given at Berlin on the 29th of April 1945 at
4:00 o'clock.   Signed: Adolf Hitler."[21]

---

[21]*Document No. 3569 of the records of the International Military Tribunal at Nuremberg.*

If one disregards Hitler's anti-Semitic obsession and the two or three notable fixations of his attitude toward the world, one sees that for Hitler ideology was nothing more than slogans. When he spoke with inner conviction about the "victorious power of the National Socialist idea," about "fanaticism" and "faith," he referred not primarily to a true intellectual image but to the party, the organization, its activity, and to his and its success. Innumerable statements made by Hitler in *Mein Kampf*, and especially in his speeches in the 1920's, provide proof that Hitler almost completely disregarded the accuracy and truth of ideological tenets. His conception and description of the ideology and the program of the NSDAP consist of clichés which are hardly original. Hitler's real interest, his total concentration and the demonical fanaticism of which he was capable were applied, instead, to questions about effectiveness, timeliness, psychological calculations, tactics, organization, and propaganda. Hitler took a position on the details of ideology and the program primarily with reference to considerations of expediency, and not out of theoretical conviction. With a candidness of which he himself was probably unaware, he called the program of the NSDAP in *Mein Kampf* a "promotion program" which "had to be so ingeniously and psychologically correct, and directed toward those without whose help even the most wonderful idea remains only an idea for all eternity." In a different section of *Mein Kampf* he speaks of "the organizational concept of an ideology," basing it on a definite unalterable dogma which alone could serve as "the instrument of a fighting nationalist ideology," and which was capable of meeting the "Marxist ideology, led by a unified elite organization." Hitler was occupied almost exclusively with questions of technical manipulation in regard to ideology and program: what to do with an idea, how to secure resonance, what kind of organization was needed for it, which points of view had to be considered.

Hitler was not very much concerned with the content of this so-called National Socialist idea and ideology, or with its explanation and consolidation, although he naturally assumed that it represented eternal, "immutable" verities. His chief consideration was the creation of a movement in competition with Marxism, equally unified and fanatical, of the same discipline and submission, and, if possible, of even greater radicalism and aggressiveness. Hitler attempted to make up for the lack of a well reasoned ideology, such as that found in Marxism, through organization and manipulation. Thomas Mann perceived this accurately when he remarked in 1933 that Nazism was the "worst Bolshevism, differentiated from the Russian version by the lack of any idea." For Hitler political belief and aggressive fanaticism were first and foremost questions of organization. Revealingly, the title of the programmatic speech which Hitler gave after the refounding of the NSDAP at the Party Rally in Weimar on 3 July 1926 was "Politics: idea and organization." Under a similar heading, "Ideology and organization," Hitler states in *Mein Kampf* the essentials about the ideology and the basic program of the NSDAP.

One has to evaluate Hitler's wooing of the masses and the workers on the basis of this expediency. The choice of methods which were politically effective rested partly on deliberation, partly on intuition. They were primarily based on the subconscious influence of the Marxism he fought, not on binding theoretical convictions. This was one of the reasons why the *völkisch* groups of agrarian and bourgeois persuasion distrusted the NSDAP. A letter by Albrecht von Graefe, the leader of the *Deutschvölkische Freiheitspartei* or DVFP (German-*Völkisch* Freedom Party), on 17 June 1925, enables one to recognize this distrust. He criticized Hitler's orientation to the left and accused the NSDAP "of wanting to make the workers the only determining factor in the *völkisch* movement." This criticism, however, was a basic misunderstanding of Hitler's thoughts. What determined Hitler's "positive" position on the proletarian question were not socialist theories and principles, but propagandistic and organizational calculations. Any attentive reader could have gathered that much by reading *Mein Kampf*. Hitler wrote:

"It is in the nature of an organization that it can only exist when the highest leadership is served by a broad, emotionally receptive mass ....From such a situation Social Democracy once drew the greatest advantage. Taking the discharged veterans, who belonged to the broadest

levels of our people and were used to discipline,
it placed them under the equally strong discipline
of the party....Our bourgeoisie always considered with disdain the fact that only the so-called
uneducated masses belonged to Marxism; it was
in fact the prerequisite for its success. While
the bourgeois parties in their one-sided intellec-
tualism were a useless, undisciplined gang,
Marxism, with its less intellectual human mate-
rial, formed an army of party soldiers, who now
obeyed the Jewish directors just as blindly as
they had once obeyed their German officers. The
German bourgeoisie, which has never concerned
itself with psychological problems...never understood that the strength of a political party
does not necessarily lie in the great and independent intelligence of its individual members, but
rather in the disciplined obedience with which
the members follow the intellectual leadership.
This is a basic consideration which we have to
keep in mind when we look into the possibility
of transforming an ideology into action....If the
nationalist idea wants to achieve complete success, it must...select certain guiding principles,
which according to their meaning and content,
evoke the support of the broad human masses,
and particularly those who guarantee the ideological fight for this idea. This is the German
proletariat."

It is evident that Hitler did not feel himself bound
to the "broad masses," the proletariat, by a feeling

of social solidarity. The improvement of the socio-economic or cultural conditions of the workers was not the impulse which convinced Hitler to form the NSDAP into a workers' and mass movement. On the contrary, he saw in the proletariat, as he understood it, primarily a vehicle and a means to an end in the struggle for power. He considered it as the truly suitable supporter of the monolithic and fanatic fighting movement which he hopefully visualized. In this view, the mass character, the social inferiority and lack of judgment which he regarded as the hallmark of the proletariat, was not a hindrance which had to be overcome, but indeed a necessary condition for success. In a two-hour speech, never published,[22] which Hitler delivered on 28 February 1926 before the *Hamburger Nationalklub* (Hamburg National Club) he explained to its bourgeois members why the NSDAP had to turn to the workers. Unlike the bourgeois party organizations the NSDAP had to appear as a fighting, fanatical mass movement. Hitler was completely forthright:

"Above all one has to make short shrift of the attitude that the masses can be satisfied with ideological concepts. Comprehension is a shaky platform for the masses. The only stable emotion is hate. It is much less susceptible to disturbance than an evaluation on the basis of scientific recognition. ... The broad mass is feminine, it knows only the harsh 'either/or'. ... The mass

[22]*HA/NSDAP, Fa 88, Fasc. 60.*

wants the man who says with a commanding voice: 'This is the right road.'... The mass must feel the triumph of its own strength, the contempt for the opponent.... Believe me, the first thing which the mass feels without any quibbling, is strength. No matter how ideal a movement is supposed to be it also has to learn to act with brutality. It must know: we fight for right, and this right will increase in the eyes of the others the stronger of purpose we appear. It is wrong (to assume) that terror drives the masses away. One can hear so-called intelligent remarks from individual workers a thousand times over. But when they are subject to mass hypnosis, this fabulous effect of their mass meetings of 200,000 people in the *Lustgarten* (park in Berlin), the individual stands like an insignificant worm among them, and these 200,000 people are for him the symbol not only of the strength, but also of the righteousness of the movement. He sees 200,000 people all of whom fight for an ideal, which he himself can not even understand, which he does not necessarily have to understand. He has a faith, and this faith is daily reinforced by its visible power.... This single-minded mass, which is infatuated with Marxism and stubbornly fights for it, is the only weapon for the movement which wants to break Marxism.''

These explanations, which can hardly be surpassed in their forthrightness, make it plain that Hitler was not primarily a *völkisch* ideologist. What motivated him was not the missionary zeal of a man who wants to spread definite ideological theories as a new way of looking at the world. We have here the fanaticism of pure aggression, which receives its aims and activity from a fixed opponent—anti-dynamicism—without a substance of its own, guided by the expediency of political dogmas and the totalitarian fighting movement. It is, in final analysis, an uncommitted fanaticism, without content, believing only in its own irresistible momentum.

Here we see the new element in the Nazi movement. The NSDAP formed by Hitler stood ideologically on the shoulders of the middle class, on the pan-German nationalists and the anti-Semitic *völkisch* sectarians of the prewar period. In style, organization, and propagandistic dynamism it was, however, avant-garde—formed by Hitler, Goebbels, and their helpers who consciously based it on the wartime and revolutionary experiences of the twentieth century. As a type of revolutionary movement, the NSDAP can be put much more easily on the same historical level as Sorel's teaching of "the use of force" and on French syndicalism. This also influenced Mussolini and fascism. It also parallels the revolutionary theory and practice of Lenin, and is not on the same historical level with the *völkisch* or conservative nationalists or bourgeoisie. Hitler's true "idea" lay in the attractiveness of the presentation, the method of campaigning, and the appeal of agitation, all of which made it possible to cover the lack of an intellectual foundation. Through these elements, as he correctly calculated, the NSDAP rapidly succeeded in leaving far behind the *völkisch* groups, which were involved in petty rivalries among themselves. Siegfried Kasche, a former *völkisch* politician and later a diplomat of the Third Reich, defended his desertion to the NSDAP in a letter to Ludendorff on 21 June 1926:[23] "I see in Hitler more of the power which forges ahead and the group more capable of fighting than I see among the Berlin gentlemen" (of the German *Völkisch* Freedom Party, the DVFP).

Kasche, the young and active propaganda chief of the Berlin-Neukölln district of the NSDAP, reported with a great show of sarcasm about the national convention of the DVFP in Berlin and on the pitiful figure cut by these rivals whom the NSDAP had passed by:

"If there has ever been a performance which passed deservedly with very little notice...it was the national convention of the DVFP....The Jewish press rightfully derided this DVFP meeting, where not a single exciting line was offered about what was to be done to save Germany. The subjects were matters of no importance: quarreling, polemics against Hitler, cries for unity, and complaints about the disgraceful condition of the treasury."[24]

---

[23]*HA/NSDAP, Fa 88, Fasc. 199.*
[24]*Complete text in "Die Anfänge der Berliner NSDAP, 1926/ 27,"* Vierteljahrshefte für Zeitgeschichte, *1960, No. 1.*

While the intellectual, ideological façade of Nazism was insignificant and worthless, its propaganda operated excellently. Hitler's leading position was without doubt based on this as well as on his genuine ability. Within the party, Hitler's demagogic gifts as an orator and his instinct for what was effective with the masses was unsurpassed. Even Goebbels' wealth of ideas and agile virtuosity fell short of Hitler's skills in this respect, while the opposition parties during the Weimar period, including the Communists, had nothing to equal Hitler. His political career within the NSDAP was almost exclusively based on his ability as a speaker and agitator. This made him the most important man in that small party of 1920, although he then held no official party position. With the dynamism of his demagogic talent, which was most effective in mass meetings, Hitler turned the simpleminded Munich club into a party of a new type: a mixture of fighting organization and a fanatical mass membership which gave the NSDAP its particular flavor. In the later phases of the development of the NSDAP, until 1933, it was Hitler personally who decided matters of propaganda and who occupied an exalted place as an election orator.

Alan Bullock, the British historian to whom we are indebted for the most thorough biography of Hitler (*Hitler—A Study in Tyranny,* revised edition: Harper, New York, 1960), probably does not go too far when he writes, "Hitler was the greatest demagogue in history." He explains with emphasis: "Those who say 'just a demagogue' fail to appreciate the nature of political power in an age of mass politics.'' Hitler and the NSDAP did not owe their sensational success to the power of an idea which appealed to the intellect. On the contrary, their triumphs were due to their non-rational activity, their aim at things closest at hand, to the agitation which resolved problems with disturbing simplicity. The originality of the party did not consist in its intellectual equipment, but in the manner in which it propagandized and fought for ideas also represented by others. It was the dynamics of the party, its parades, the ceremonial blessing of banners, the marching columns of the SA, the uniforms, the bands, etc., which captured the imagination of the masses.

There was no lack of observers, even during the Weimar period, who clearly discerned that the strength of the NSDAP lay in its behavior and in its methods of propaganda. Arthur Mahraun, the leader of the *Jungdeutscher Orden* (Young German Order),[25] wrote after the fantastic election success of the Nazi party on 14 September 1930:

> ''The leaders of this party have understood how to turn the disgust of the German people over the deep economic depression into the wheels which drive the mills of the Party. The fathers of Marxism never achieved the skill in the manipulation which the men around Goebbels used to

[25]*Translator's note: The* Jungdeutscher Orden *was a significant conservative-bourgeois group of young people who belatedly joined one of the disintegrating Liberal parties at the time of the Nazi landslide of the early 1930's.*

make the most of the emotions of the masses....
The Nazis are allowed to say anything. They
are permitted to appear before princes and
nobility, with former November criminals[26] and
former Marxists. These applaud them. They
believe in the miracle of radicalism. They
believe in the dictatorship which is supposed to
save Germany."

One of those who recognized the modern nature of
Nazi propaganda methods quite early, was the writer
Friedrich Franz von Unruh. In a study of Nazism
which he published in 1931, he observed:

"All propaganda, according to Hitler, has to
limit its intellectual level to the understanding of
the most stupid among its audience. Banal 'Black
against White!' rather than intricate thoughts—no
scruples about doing the opponent wrong...how
silly can you get? Truth is not at stake, success
is. Success came. Suddenly the number of seats
in the Reichstag had increased eightfold. Germany
held her breath, the world listened. And the
Nazis? They acted according to the principle:
'After a victory, prepare for battle.'
They planned 70,000 meetings after the victory

---

[26]*Translator's note: "November criminals" - referring to November 1918 - was the epithet attached by nationalist agitators
to the opposition parties and politicians who took over responsibility from the collapsing monarchy and were accused of having had a hand in the fall of the old regime.*

at the polls. Again an avalanche passed across
the Reich. Again and again it is proved how
dependably the campaign apparatus functions. A
plan of mobilization unfolds. Town after town,
village after village is invaded.... General staff
and propaganda expert march together. Direction
and organization are the most modern, propaganda
is centralized, an emblem which is powerfully impressive, the swastika, is used in small and
mammoth sizes, on flags, banners and official
seals, also on campaign buttons. All agitation is
uniform and hard-hitting, starting with the ar-
rangement of posters (size, color, text, printing)
in all their detail....Newspapers also play a
part, although they are now in the background,
in contrast to the other parties....(Success)
comes only from *speeches*, the spoken not the
printed word.... The writer, Hitler explained,
does not know his public. He lacks psychological
finesse. Only the speaker can see whether the
listener is caught.... The theme must be explosive
...and contain accusations, reproaches, demands.
No wisdom from the council table. Stir up anger
and passion and stoke the fire until the crowd
goes berserk."[27]

This kind of propaganda often led to active violence,
or terror, as a demonstration of power. Hitler was
convinced that such violence stimulates the masses

[27]*Friedrich Franz von Unruh*, Nationalsozialismus, *Frankfurt,
1931, p. 16ff.*

more than any attempt to convince them by an appeal to their intelligence. From the moment Hitler determined the policy of the NSDAP, the party followed this prescription. Provocations and scandals, and meetings where "things happened" made the NSDAP a local attraction in Munich, even before 1920. In a 1922 report by the Bavarian Ministry of the Interior regarding the NSDAP, we find the following evaluation:

> "One can assume as common knowledge that the National Socialist Party, although it calls itself a party for reconstruction, pursues the political fight with such vehemence and passion that it does not stop at anything....In addition to this, the tone of the party press, the tenor of its pamphlets and advertising, the terroristic assaults on rival meetings, the attacks on other persons, the desecration of buildings and parks are widely known. One can scarcely think of anything more violent and passionate than their attacks against political opponents."[28]

Besides Hitler, Goebbels too understood how to put the NSDAP "in the limelight" through the use of provocations and spectacular activities. The best example of this is the "battle for Red Berlin" which he began when he was appointed Gauleiter of the NSDAP in Berlin (Brandenburg) in November 1926. Before the arrival of Goebbels in Berlin, the NSDAP groups and the SA, which had existed for some time,

[28]*HA/NSDAP, Fa 88, Fasc. 99.*

were almost completely without influence and reputation. Only a few hundred party comrades constituted
the core of the Berlin NSDAP in July 1926. Personal
quarrels among the leaders of the party district had
raised the "acute danger of the complete collapse of
the Berlin organization of the NSDAP," an intra-party
report of October 1926 noted.[29] Within three to four
months, Goebbels succeeded in making the NSDAP
the political talk of the town, the object of attacks in
the press. Repressive acts by the police were followed
by the first prohibition of the party. Despite the
temporary outlawing of the NSDAP in Berlin (May
1927 to March 1928) the goal had been reached.
Goebbels accomplished this partly through the reorganization of the SA and the SS and the formation
of the first Hitler Youth groups, but especially by a
series of mass meetings, by carefully planned meeting
hall brawls and fights with the Communists in the
Wedding district and other "red sections" of Berlin.
Goebbels lifted the NSDAP from obscurity to importance and recognition. His actions deliberately
produced its first few martyrs, thereby providing the
party with a martyr complex and increasing the
members' fanaticism.

The fact that the "victory march of the Nazi ideas"
was in reality the organizational work of *Putschists*
and terrorists, is made plain by a report of February
1927 of Reinhold Muchow, who worked for Goebbels
as a propaganda and organizational expert. The
report refers to the first planned collision, of 11

[29]*See the article cited in note 24.*

February 1927, with the Communist Party in the Wedding district. Muchow wrote that it would not be too much to say "...that, for instance, the Stuttgart, the Weimar, or the Hamburg SA would receive quite a beating from the Communists if they were dispatched to Berlin. These SA groups would lack everything which here belongs to the daily modern political battle for power: a knowledge of the battlefield and methods of warfare, tactics, merciless attack (even if it should lead to death), calculation, and cunning brazenness—in short, ways and means which are typical of Berlin."

Thus, in street brawls and angry interruptions of meetings, the Berlin Nazis perfected their techniques for disturbing the public peace and for attracting attention to their cause.

4. National Socialism and the Totalitarian Society

The preceding discussion concerning the relations between *völkisch* ideology and the Nazi organization has given a preliminary answer to the question about the socialist character of the NSDAP and what Hitler thought of the workers. Hitler decided on the organization of a "labor movement" not out of any humanitarian considerations or for purposes of a socialist reorganization of society, but in cynical calculation of the psychology of the masses. Hitler was attracted to the proletariat because it constituted a socially and psychologically available quantity of energy, useful for the struggle for political power, not as a part of society whose interests were especially important to him. However, one has to consider the axiom that there is no such thing as an ideology of complete deception. Ideology and political programs, even if their originators intended them for purely propagandistic purposes, become reality to the extent to which they are held to be true, are believed, and are taken seriously as principles. Without a doubt, therefore, for a part of the NSDAP and its followers, the slogans of Nazism and the people's community *(Volksgemeinschaft)* which were part of the NSDAP's slogans, were more than mere propaganda.

Aside from *völkisch* resentments and anti-Semitic feelings of envy and hate, the anticapitalist longing during the fighting period of the NSDAP was undoubtedly one of its most powerful political-ideological impulses. It was certainly not its worst. The Nazis avoided a clear stand in the programmatic statements of the party and of its representatives regarding economic and social-political questions and the matter of socialization. Though one could interpret these utterances as a conservative-bourgeois attempt to safeguard property, it was nevertheless true that the party program, the "Twenty-five Points" of 24 February 1920, contained a number of unquestionably revolutionary or socialistic demands.

Hitler declared in 1926 that the program was not subject to any change whatsoever. "Nationalization of trusts" (Point 13), "Profit sharing of the workers in large-scale industrial undertakings" (Point 14), "Transfer of department stores to communal ownership" (Point 16), "Carrying out of land reform" (Point 17)—all of these were undoubtedly directed against private industry, capital, chain stores, and the big landowner. Hitler's additional remarks in *Mein Kampf* about the way in which the party program of 1920 was formulated make it clear that a revolutionary, *völkisch* mass movement simply had no chance in 1920 without concessions to the left. For example, he emphasized the necessity "of choosing certain slogans which are designed, in nature and content, to command adherence by broad masses of people" and especially by "the German proletariat," because it "alone guarantees the ideological success of this idea." During the early days of the NSDAP, the anticapitalist aims and propaganda received considerable support from representatives of the party, although to a lesser degree from Hitler personally. The idea of socialism on a national basis, the concept of a socialist community of the people, of a specifically German socialism somewhere between the communism exemplified by Russian Bolshevism and the capitalism of the victorious Western powers, became after 1918 an important and persuasive intellectual political beacon. This proved to be an advantage to the NSDAP; the party name itself mirrors the mood of the times. For a while the idea of a "national" socialism played some part in almost all intellectual and political camps of the period after the First World War: it was important to the liberal followers of Friedrich Naumann, who in the 1880's and 1890's attempted to bring about democratization and the removal of the feudal

governing hierarchy via the Imperial welfare state.
Among conservatives, the German nationalist and the
Christian-democratic ideas of the Stöcker movement
of the 1880's were still very much alive. They received
renewed impetus through the young-conservative
movement led by Moeller van den Bruck and others,
as well as through Spengler's impressive formula,
"Prussianism and Socialism." In the ranks of the
Social Democrats, the disappointments over the inef-
fectiveness of the Second International during the
First World War, and the missed opportunity at
social revolution in 1918, caused people like August
Winnig and Otto Strasser to become the pathfinders
for National Socialist concepts. These ideas even
affected the radical left, consisting of the Independent
Socialists and Communists. From these ranks Ernst
Niekisch appeared with his national and social revolutionary program. The propaganda value of the
NSDAP slogan, "the common good before individual
gain," must be understood on the basis of this
widespread desire. This was felt by the best intellectual
and political talents of the 1920's who saw in the idea
of a "national" socialism the resolution of the
historical German antagonism between "national"
and "socialist", although with varying theoretical
justifications and practical conclusions.

Aside from the narrow circle of the Munich group
around Hitler, there emerged a pronounced socialist
wing in the Nazi party. Such men as Hermann Esser,
Alfred Rosenberg, and Julius Streicher were anti-
capitalists only when "Jewish high finance" and

"Jewish capital" were involved. They interpreted
Feder's thesis of the "breaking of interest slavery,"
by submerging socialism in anti-Semitism. The foremost representatives of the NSDAP "Socialists" were
Gregor Strasser, the Party leader of Lower Bavaria
(1921-1923), and his brother Otto Strasser, who
joined the National Socialist movement in 1924. The
temporary elimination of Hitler, after the putsch of
9 November 1923, brought out for the first time the
opposition among the remaining members of the party.
Between the Strasser wing and the group around
Rosenberg, Esser, and Streicher, no agreement was
achieved. The two factions went their separate ways
in 1924. Until Hitler refounded the NSDAP in February
1925, the Strasser brothers determined the policy of
the National Socialist Freedom Movement which
existed primarily in Lower Bavaria, but also in
Central Germany.

In the beginning of 1925 Hitler succeeded in getting
the Strasser brothers to leave the National Socialist
Freedom Movement and to return to the reorganized
NSDAP. In return he had to concede them far-reaching
independence, at least partially necessitated by or-
dinances passed in the spring of 1925 prohibiting
public speaking by Hitler in most parts of Germany.
In some parts he was not allowed to speak until
1927-1928. In particular, he had to concede to the
Strassers the North German area where the NSDAP
began to establish a foothold in 1925, almost entirely
through Strasser supporters. Hitler soon succeeded
both in preventing the North German Gauleiter from

achieving a key position in the organization, and in destroying the Strasser domain in North Germany through a policy of personal intrigue. But the fact remains that until the beginning of the 1930's there remained an unbridgeable chasm between the strongly social-revolutionary North German NSDAP and the Munich party leadership. The bimonthly *National-sozialistische Briefe* which Gregor Strasser started in October 1925 in Elberfeld, as well as the weeklies *Der Nationale Sozialist* and the *Berliner Arbeiterzeitung*, which were issued from 1926 to 1930 by Strasser's publishing house, the *Kampfverlag*, were at that time the most important propaganda organs of the NSDAP in Northern Germany. These publications were ideologically much closer to the Christian Socialists, to the right wing of the Social Democrats, to the unions, or to the individual national-revolutionary and national-bolshevik groups, than to the nordic-Aryan ideological metaphysics and morality which Rosenberg advocated in the *Völkischer Beobachter*. In the matter of individual political questions of immediate impact, the difference between Hitler and the socialists in the NSDAP was apparent. The socialists, despite their fantastic doctrines, were seriously concerned about social questions and dealt with them with revolutionary zeal. For example, in 1926, the Strasser group, together with the Communist and Socialist parties, rejected the reimbursement of the nobility for their expropriation. A letter of 22 May 1925 to Hitler by a leader of a National Socialist youth group exemplifies the ideological dilemma and ambiguity of the NSDAP during the 1920's:

"We have created a youth group of the NSDAP in Köln-Mühlheim which is one of the best in the whole Rhineland. I would like to inform the Party leadership that among the thoughtful members more and more voices are supporting a transfer to the KPD. Daily we see how the *German* employer ignores the demands of the times with unscrupulous disregard and degrades to animals those who help him to gain wealth....It is absolutely wrong to make a difference between Jewish and non-Jewish capitalism. That is the reproach which thinking workers are making again and again—and with complete justification ....We must become a real workers' party, otherwise the whole movement will fail....Does the NSDAP know that rapacious finance capital can only be fought on an international basis, that the 'breaking of interest slavery' also can only be solved by international rules? How then do our aims differ from those of the Communists?"[30]

Similar to the urban-industrial Rhine-Ruhr area, there existed a distinctly socialist center of the NSDAP in Berlin during the 1920's, which followed more or less consciously the example set by the KPD (Communist Party) in questions of organization and propaganda methods. It was characteristic that Goebbels, who belonged to the Strasser wing of the NSDAP at this time, should have chosen as a theme for the first Nazi mass meeting in Berlin-Wedding,

[30]*HA/NSDAP, Fa 88, Fasc. 335.*

"The Collapse of the Bourgeois Class State." Other
parties, the German Nationalist Party, the German
People's Party and the Democrats conducted their
1928 election campaigns against the NSDAP in Berlin
and North Germany by pointing to the "program of
class struggle" and to the revolutionary socialistic
demands of the National Socialists.

As long as Hitler stuck to the revolutionary course
of the NSDAP and the idea of a National Socialist
seizure of power by force, after the Italian fascist
model, he could ill afford to take a decisive stand
against the socialist wing of the NSDAP. He needed
to keep alive the revolutionary fighting spirit of the
NSDAP and the SA. In Berlin, and in the other large
cities workers and many unemployed made up the
original membership of the SA. As long as the NSDAP
was a party involved only in agitation and was nowhere
forced to put its propaganda to the practical test,
the ideological discrepancies between its left and
right wing could easily be hidden. During 1929-1930
this situation changed. Hitler pursued a basic change
of course after the success of the NSDAP in local
elections: an absolute National Socialist majority in
the Coburg city council in the election of 23 June 1929;
the appointment of the first National Socialist minister,
Dr. Wilhelm Frick, in Thuringia after the state
election of 8 December 1929; and finally the sensational
gain of almost 6.5 million votes (18% of the total), and
with it 108 seats in the Reichstag election of 14
September 1930; and the simultaneous entry of National
Socialists into the cabinet of the state of Brunswick.
Gaining power through elections now became Hitler's
aim.

The new course was emphasized by an oath to adhere to legal means for winning power, made by Hitler during the public trial in Ulm of three National Socialist officers of the German army. After this commenced the unveiled flirtation of the NSDAP with the Heinrich Brüning government, with the nationalist right wing (as in the Harzburg Front with the German Nationalist Party of Hugenberg), with big industry, as represented by Hugo Stinnes and Fritz Thyssen, with the financial world of Emil Georg von Stauss, Hjalmar Schacht, and Kurt von Schröder, and with the army and the big landholders. Thus, a conflict with the socialist wing of the NSDAP and the SA, which had been trained for revolution and war to gain power, became virtually unavoidable. The break between Hitler and Otto Strasser in May 1930, the resignation of the then highest SA leader Pfeffer von Salomon, Hitler's assumption in the autumn of 1930 of the supreme leadership of the SA, with Ernst Röhm as chief of staff, and the so-called Stennes putsch of the Berlin and East German SA, on 1 April 1931, were the overt signs of these diametrically opposed points of view.

Otto Strasser then published a report, which may be accepted as essentially authentic, of his two-day discussion with Hitler on 21-22 May 1930 in Berlin; this was the cause for the final separation.[31] In this document, Strasser describes in detail the differences of opinion which existed between Hitler and himself. Strasser reveals that after he criticized Hitler's

[31]*Otto Strasser*. Ministersessel oder Revolution *(Cabinet Minister or Revolution), Berlin, 1930.*

rejection of socialism in the interest of co-operation
with the bourgeois right as the main reason for the
disagreement, Hitler replied:

> "What you mean by socialism is nothing more
> than the crassest Marxism. Look here, the great
> mass of the workers want nothing more than
> bread and circuses; it has no understanding for
> any kind of ideals. We want a select new ruling
> class, which is not motivated by any kind of
> morality of compassion, as you are, but convinced
> that it has the right to rule because of its better
> race, and which maintains without scruples this
> rule over the broad masses."

According to Strasser, Hitler also opposed the theory
of co-operative ownership by workers of the estab-
lishments in which they worked, and he remarked:

> "With what right do these people demand part
> ownership or even participation in the manage-
> ment?... The entrepreneur, who is responsible
> for production, provides bread for the workers
> .... The owners reached the top because of their
> ability... which again proves them to be of a
> higher race, and they have the right to lead."

It was not difficult for Strasser to show that the
application of racial and biological theory regarding
the right of the stronger to dominate society had no
relation to the idea of a national socialism. He saw
in socialism an integration of the nation in its totality

and the overcoming of the differences between the economically stronger and the weaker.

Fourteen days after this discussion, the split was complete. With the agreement of his supporters, Herbert Blank, Bruno Buchrucker, Eugen Mossakowsky, and other North German leaders of the NSDAP, Otto Strasser published on 4 June 1930 the pamphlet "The Socialists Leave the NSDAP," the founding manifesto of his own organization, the *Kampfgemeinschaft revolutionärer Nationalsozialisten* (Fighting Union of Revolutionary National Socialists). Out of this organization developed the *Schwarze Front* (Black Front). The Nazi secret police devoted considerable effort to its persecution.

Otto Strasser's challenge, which was followed three years later by the break between his brother Gregor and Hitler, was a symptom of the continuously deteriorating relationship between the SA and the political leadership of the NSDAP. This dispute found additional expression in the conversion of individual National Socialists to the Communist Party. This took place with increasing frequency and the converts were evidently seeking an uncompromising revolutionary position toward the Weimar Republic and the present society. One of these converts was Lieutenant Richard Scheringer, who had become well known during the Ulm trial. On 18 March 1931, in a public declaration which was also read in the Reichstag, Scheringer resigned from the NSDAP and entered the KPD. This was especially embarrassing because Scheringer had been celebrated by the Nazi press as a martyr of the National Socialist movement only six months earlier.

Letters in which Scheringer justified his step were later published.[32] In one of these letters he wrote:

> "My aim is and remains the national and social liberation of the German people. My path led me to the NSDAP because I saw in it an organization which united all revolutionary elements in preparation for revolutionary war, especially through winning the workers. The policy of the National Socialist leadership and discussions with Hitler, Goebbels, Röhm, Frank, and others during the past months, convinced me that the NSDAP can not bring about liberation because it has entered a clearly reactionary and capitalistic course."

A very similar basic tendency was the criticism displayed by the SA leaders who left the NSDAP, together with Walter Stennes, and formed the *National-sozialistische Kampfbewegung Deutschlands*, or NSKD (National Socialist Fighting Movement of Germany), in the spring of 1931, and temporarily joined Otto Strasser's Fighting Union. One of these SA leaders wrote to Hitler in April 1931:

> "You have lost the right to continue to call yourself 'leader and founder' of a movement which

---

[32]*Erwachendes Volk. Briefe an Leutnant Scheringer (Awakening People. Letters to Lieutenant Scheringer), Berlin, 1931. See also Scheringer's autobiography: Das Grosse Los unter Soldaten, Bauern und Rebellen (The Great Sweepstake among Soldiers, Peasants and Rebels), Hamburg, 1959.*

is holy to us, because you have degraded yourself into a manager or lawyer of a NSDAP club. The NSDAP, like all other parties, serves only for the preservation of a bunch of bloodsuckers. We are not a handful of mutineers...but honest fighters against the betrayal of National Socialism."[33]

This process of erosion within the revolutionary wing of the NSDAP continued during the following years. The majority of the originally socialist followers among those of Hitler's close circle slowly changed their attitudes and did not follow the example of the Strasser brothers. This was true of Goebbels, and of quite a number of provincial party chiefs like Martin Mutschmann of Saxony or Robert Ley in the Rhineland. Ley later became the successor of Gregor Strasser as *Organisationsleiter* (head of the Political Organization) of the Party and leader of the *Deutsche Arbeitsfront* or DAF (German Labor Front) in the Third Reich. The socialist tendency inside the NSDAP played a significant part into the years 1933-1934. It had a special center in Berlin, where in 1928 the *Betriebszellenorganisation* or NSBO (National Socialist Factory Cell Organization) had been founded to win over the predominantly Social Democratic and Communist-oriented workers in the factories. The nature of the following they sought compelled the NSBO to follow an unequivocal leftist course if it wanted to penetrate the cells of workers organized in the independent unions or in the Communist

[33]*HA/NSDAP, Fa 88, Fasc. 83.*

revolutionary unions. Reinhold Muchow, the organizational creator of the NSBO, who had the support of Gregor Strasser, was an exponent of this course. In a pamphlet entitled "Are the National Socialists Social Reactionaries?" (1931), Muchow categorically denied that the NSDAP intended to destroy the unions. "We National Socialists and the *völkisch* conscious workers," he wrote, "will resist all attacks against the existence of the unions." He acknowledged just as emphatically the use of the economic strike as the "trenchant weapon" of the workers. He protested, "We National Socialists will support with all our power all justified economic strikes in the future." He rejected as absolutely incorrect the assertion that the National Socialists would, after they came to power, do away with the workers' councils, and with labor codetermination or collective bargaining.

Two or three years later all that Muchow had so categorically denied did happen. May Day had been raised by the Nazis in 1933 to the status of a legal "day of national labor." It was celebrated with parades and gigantic displays of fireworks on the Tempelhof Field in Berlin to show the love of the government for the workers. One day later, on 2 May, all over Germany came the carefully prepared assault. The offices and houses of the General German Trade Union Federation (ADGB) were occupied by the SA and the SS and the treasuries were confiscated. The most important trade union leaders, such as Theodor Leipart and Peter Grassmann, were arrested. Following swiftly in the steps of the coercive measures against the free unions came the "voluntary" disbanding, under suitable pressures, of the Christian trade unions and of the nationalist unions of white collar workers. With their disappearance every independent economic organization and group representing the interests of the German workers had been extinguished.

The "law for the reorganization of national labor" of 24 January 1934 abolished the workers' councils, as well as collective bargaining. The role of the independently elected shop stewards was taken by the so-called *Vertrauensräte* (grievance men) who were appointed by agreement between management and the representative of the NSBO. State-appointed labor arbitrators subordinate to the Labor Ministry had the right to enter labor disputes, and they were ultimately responsible for the determination of the wage rates which now took the place of voluntary collective bargaining arrangements.

Muchow and his followers in the NSBO believed, in 1933, that they could at least save some independent organization for the wage earners within the social order of the Third Reich. Within the framework of the experiments undertaken to create a corporative state, they hoped to maintain an inclusive organization of wage earners as the successor to the independent trade unions, and to use it as a counterweight to the power of management. Yet, not even this succeeded. The NSBO quickly lost all its influence. The mammoth organization of the German Labor Front, which had been formed out of the remains of the unions in May 1933, sank to the level of a Nazi indoctrination and propaganda institution, and took on the features of

an enormous entertainment and welfare organization, by offering the programs of *Kraft durch
Freude* (Strength through Joy) and *Schönheit der
Arbeit* (Beauty of Labor). These two programs served
as a surrogate of democracy and "organized joy of
life," as Ernst Niekisch put it. The siren song of
special welfare state benefits or the efficient manipulation of "fringe benefits" by the employer were
used here with the deliberation and unscrupulous
effectiveness of a totalitarian state. The independent
worker found himself systematically degraded to the
level of the "broad masses," of which Hitler had
always wanted him to be a part. He was given the
social prestige of the leisure class, as for instance
by his participation in tours to Scandinavia at reduced
prices. Factory celebrations and free entertainment
kept him in a good mood.

Reinhold Muchow was the victim of an accident in
the autumn of 1933. Other insubordinate leaders of
the old NSBO with its social-revolutionary attitude—
among them Walter Schuhmann, Ludwig Brucker,
and O. E. Krüger—were set aside in August 1934.
Ley, the leader of the German Labor Front, declared
hypocritically at the 1937 Nuremberg Party Rally:
"The NSBO was ideologically wrong, as were the
unions. It did not fit into our National Socialist
orientation." No part of the old socialist program
ever became reality, not even the nationalization of
the department stores for which members of the petty
bourgeois middle class within the NSDAP had fought
so vigorously. An announcement by Hitler's deputy
Rudolf Hess, made on 7 July 1933, postponed this

matter "until later," to be forgotten forever. The National Socialist *Kampfbund des Handels und Gewerbes, NS-Hago* (NS Militant Association of Commerce and the Trades), which was headed by the middle class economist Theodor von Renteln, had still used the Nazi seizure of power for local attacks on department stores, chain stores and consumers' co-operatives. It was dissolved in the spring of 1933, even before the NSBO ceased to function. Some undaunted Nazi social theorists continued to hope for two more years that a new type of people's community would develop as a result of the much-discussed "corporative structure." Its adherents envisioned a social order consisting of autonomous chambers, each composed of a special economic or social group, which would be endowed with legislative initiative in economic matters. Fritz Thyssen, the representative of big industry and a long-time financial supporter of the NSDAP, was a disciple of Othmar Spann's theories of a corporative society. Hitler allowed him to establish an *Institut für Ständewesen* (Institute for Corporative Structure) in Düsseldorf which he had to finance himself.[34] Thyssen had joined the NSDAP, as did others who agreed with Spann, because Point 25 of the Party program provided for the "formation of *Stände- und Berufskammern* (corporative and professional chambers) in the several federal states for the execution of laws passed by the Reich." In 1933 a special department under Dr. Max Frauendorfer was established in the German Labor Front for planning

---

[34]*Fritz Thyssen.* I Paid Hitler, *New York/Toronto, 1941.*

a corporative state. Yet nothing but inconsequential and confused plans came of these various efforts.

Late in 1934, Hitler ordered a halt to all attempts to bring about a reorganization of the economy on a corporative basis. This caused great disappointment among the disciples of Spann in the ranks of the intellectual followers of the NSDAP and among other idealistic-romantic ideologists who believed in an "organic, corporatively organized national community" in place of the "mechanically democratic class society." The bodies which functioned as the *Reichsnährstand* (Reich Food Corporation), or as *Reichsstand des Deutschen Handwerks und Handels* (Reich Corporation of German Trades and Commerce) in the German Labor Front were little more than corporative nomenclature.

Frauendorfer's goal of a corporative state, as set forth in a 1933 brochure, "The Corporative Idea in National Socialism," was not realized. The economic and social life was not to be based on the representation of independent trade unions or professional bodies. Nor was an economic sphere free of politics contemplated which would have had independent ways of resolving social and economic conflicts. Instead the social organization of the Third Reich was to be determined by the pre-eminence of the totalitarian state party over all professional, economic and social life.

In place of a horizontal grouping of spontaneous social forces, the Nazis subordinated all professional groups, all trades and all branches of the economy to the party and the state it ruled. Just as Hitler had once formed the NSDAP and its associated organizations into one unified militant movement, so after 1933 the guiding principle was the mobilization of the whole nation into one unceasing, dynamic movement. A network of party auxiliaries, such as the *Nationalsozialistischer Verband* or NSV (National Socialist Auxiliary Association) and the *Nationalsozialistischer Kraftfahrer Korps* or NSKK (National Socialist Motor Corps) and the Hitler Youth, organized the whole population into an all-inclusive marching column. A smoothly working propaganda machine hammered into the head of every member of the nation the image of the leader and his devoted followers, as well as the need for ever-renewed efforts.

Professional and social groups found themselves drawn into continuous dynamic action, even if their participation was only vicarious via Nazi propaganda. The Nazi organization of the legal profession received the label "Legal Front" which "marched" next to the Labor Front. The various stages for providing work became "battles for employment," and job training and the workers' increase in production took the form of contests. In addition, there was a constant fare of national holidays, proclamations, mass rallies, acts of state, and Führer speeches. Every single person was addressed according to his particular perspective and was psychologically fitted to be a particle in the great activated mass of his national community.

Hitler, Goebbels, and their aides demonstrated their abilities as brilliant promotion experts in the way in which they staged national celebrations.

Examples of these skills are the Peasants' Rally at
Bückeberg, the spectacularly organized Olympic
Games of 1936, or the annual gigantic effort of the
Nuremberg Party Rally, paraded in front of the
scenery of newly constructed colossal buildings. They
ably mixed monumental pomp with folksy touches,
sports exhibits with military exactness, sentimental
theatrical displays with stately pageantry, and thereby
skillfully played on the heartstrings of typically
German feelings.

National Socialism did not create a reorganization
or a new type of society, as the socialists or the
disciples of the corporative idea of the movement
had expected. It did succeed in absorbing almost
all social life through the multifarious channels of
the party. The party itself constituted the new social
order which took control, assigned roles and functions
and subjected the individual in his social and professional life to the purposes of the party. The new
frame of reference obviously reduced the old social
contrasts between employer and employee, and between
the old middle class and finance capital. Many persons
living in the Third Reich erroneously interpreted the
change as a step toward an egalitarian "people's
community" with a common purpose. The illusion of
a community was created by cleverly arranged and
dramatic measures such as the *Winterhilfswerk*
(Winter Aid) and other appeals to make sacrifices,
by camouflaging the social differences which continued
to exist between workers, white collar employees,
and employers, with new egalitarian slogans such as
Arbeiter der Stirn und der Faust (Workers of the

brain and the fist), and by raising the social prestige
of the agrarian population by semantically promoting
it to *Nährstand* (The estate of the food producers).

The Third Reich provided ample proof that a people
almost totally dominated and harnessed in the service
of totalitarianism can be manipulated to the point
where it will welcome domination and believe it is
one happy national community. National Socialist
ideology and propaganda succeeded in convincing the
public that Nazi resentments and phobias represented
the sound instincts of the people, and that its un-
reasoning mob psychology was genuine and *"völkisch."*
The Hitler state succeeded in characterizing the state
of unreflecting intoxication, the renunciation of individual judgment and individual will as the highest form
of sacrifice and of selflessness of a "people's
community." The basis for this thinking was a
willingness for self-effacement, for complete devotion
to an imagined historic greatness and future potential,
worth the sacrifice of individual self-interest as well
as of any sense of responsibility.

National Socialism was the expression of totalitarianism which drew on the pathology of a modern
mass society in which the individual had lost his ties
and values and all sense of direction. National
Socialism in Germany became the sinister embodiment
of a dynamic nihilism devoid of ideological commitment.

Selected Bibliography

PART I. WORKS IN ENGLISH.
Prepared by Kurt Rosenbaum.

Baumont, M. et al. *The Third Reich.* New York: Praeger, 1955.

Boehm, Eric H. *We Survived.* New Haven: Yale University Press, 1949.

Bullock, Alan. *Hitler: A Study in Tyranny.* Rev. ed., New York: Harper and Row, 1962.

Butler, Rohan. *The Roots of National Socialism, 1783-1933.* London: Faber, 1941.

Crankshaw, E. *Gestapo: Instrument of Tyranny.* New York: Viking, 1956.

Deuel, Wallace. *People Under Hitler.* New York: Harcourt, Brace, 1943.

Dulles, Allen W. *Germany's Underground.* New York: Macmillan, 1947.

Ebenstein, William. *The Nazi State.* New York: Farrar and Rinehart, 1943.

Gisevius, H. Bernd. *To the Bitter End.* Boston: Houghton Mifflin, 1947.

The Goebbels Diaries, 1942-1943, edited, translated, and with an introduction by Louis P. Lochner. Garden City: Doubleday, 1948.

Hale, Oron J. *The Captive Press in the Third Reich.* Princeton: Princeton University Press, 1964.

Hassell, Ulrich von. *The Von Hassell Diaries, 1938-1944.* New York: Doubleday, 1947.

Heiber, H. (ed.). *The Early Goebbels Diaries, 1925-1926.* New York: Praeger, 1963.

Heiden, Konrad. *A History of National Socialism.* New York: Knopf, 1935.

Heiden, Konrad. *Der Fuehrer: Hitler's Rise to Power.* Boston: Houghton Mifflin, 1944.

Höss, Rudolf. *Commandant in Auschwitz.* New York: World, 1960.

Hofer, Walther. *War Premeditated, 1939.* London: Thames and Hudson, 1955. (English translation from *Die Entfesselung des zweiten Weltkrieges.*)

Jarman, T. L. *The Rise and Fall of Nazi Germany.* New York: New York University Press, 1956.

Klemperer, K. von. *Germany's New Conservatism.* Princeton: Princeton University Press, 1957.

Kogon, Eugen. *The Theory and Practice of Hell: The German Concentration Camps and the System Behind Them.* New York: Farrar, Straus, and Cudahy, 1951.

Kohn, Hans. *The Mind of Germany: The Education of a Nation.* New York: Scribner's, 1960.

Kubizek, August. *The Young Hitler I Knew.* Boston: Houghton Mifflin, 1955.

Leber, A. *Conscience in Revolt: Sixty-four Stories of Resistance in Germany, 1933-1945.* London: Valentine, Mitchell, 1957.

Lerner, D. *The Nazi Elite.* Stanford: Stanford University Press, 1951.

Mayer, Milton S. *They Thought They Were Free: The Germans, 1933-1945.* Chicago: University of Chicago Press, 1955.

Meinecke, Friedrich. *The German Catastrophe.* Translated by S. Fay. Cambridge: Harvard University Press, 1950.

Mosse, G. L. *The Crisis of German Ideology: Intellectual Origins of the Third Reich.* New York: Grosset and Dunlap, 1964.

Neumann, Franz L. *Behemoth: The Structure and Practice of National Socialism.* New York: Oxford University Press, 1942.

Rauschning, Hermann. *The Revolution of Nihilism.* New York: Longmans, Green, 1939.

Reitlinger, Gerald. *SS—Alibi of a Nation, 1922-1945.* New York: Viking Press, 1957.

Rothfels, Hans. *The German Opposition to Hitler.* Hinsdale, Illinois: Regnery, 1948.

Schumann, F. L. *The Nazi Dictatorship.* 2nd ed., New York: Knopf, 1939.

Stern, F. *The Politics of Cultural Despair.* Berkeley: University of California Press, 1961.

Strasser, Otto. *Hitler and I.* Boston: Houghton Mifflin, 1940.

Thyssen, Fritz. *I Paid Hitler.* New York: Farrar and Rinehart, 1941.

Trevor-Roper, H. R. *The Last Days of Hitler.* New York: Macmillan, 1947.

Viereck, P. *Metapolitics: The Roots of the Nazi Mind.* New York: Putnam's, 1960.

Vogt, H. *The Burden of Guilt: A Short History of Germany, 1914-1945.* Translated by H. Strauss; introduction by G. A. Craig. New York: Oxford University Press, 1964.

Wilmot, Chester. *The Struggle for Europe.* New York: Harper, 1952.

PART II. WORKS IN GERMAN
This bibliography appeared in the original work by Broszat.

Adler, H. G. *Theresienstadt, 1941-1945. Das Antlitz einer Zwangsgemeinschaft. Geschichte, Soziologie, Psychologie.* Tübingen, 1955.

Baeyer-Katte, Wanda von. *Das Zerstörende in der Politik.* Heidelberg, 1957.

Bracher, Karl Dietrich. *Die Auflösung der Weimarer Republik.* 2nd ed., Stuttgart, 1958.

Buchheim, Hans. *Das Dritte Reich.* Munich, 1958.

Celovsky, Boris. *Das Münchener Abkommen 1938.* Stuttgart, 1958.

Conrad, Walter. *Der Kampf um die Kanzeln. Erinnerungen und Dokumente aus der Hitlerzeit.* Berlin, 1957.

Dallin, Alexander. *Deutsche Herrschaft in Russland.* Düsseldorf, 1958.

Diels, Rudolf. *Lucifer ante portas. Es spricht der erste Chef der Gestapo.* Stuttgart, 1949.

Erdmann, Karl-Dietrich. *Die Zeit der Weltkriege (Bruno Gebhardt: Handbuch der Dt. Geschichte,* Bd. IV.). Stuttgart, 1959.

Foertsch, Hermann. *Schuld und Verhängnis. Die Fritsch-Krise im Frühjahr 1938 als Wendepunkt in der Geschichte der nationalsozialistischen Zeit.* Stuttgart, 1951.

Greiner, Helmuth. *Die Oberste Wehrmachtführung 1939-1943. Nach dem Kriegstagebuch des Wehrmachtsführungsstabes.* Wiesbaden, 1951.

Graml, Hermann. *Der 9. November 1938. "Reichskristallnacht".* Bonn, 1953.

Grebing, Helga. *Der Nationalsozialismus. Ursprung und Wesen.* Munich, 1959.

Hallgarten, George W. F. *Hitler, Reichswehr und Industrie. Zur Geschichte der Jahre 1918-1933.* Frankfurt, 1955.

Hassell, Ulrich von. *Vom anderen Deutschland. Aus nachgelassenen Tagebüchern der Jahre 1938-1944.* Freiburg and Zurich, 1946.

Heiden, Konrad. *Die Geburt des Dritten Reiches. Die Geschichte des Nationalsozialismus bis Herbst 1933.* Zurich, 1934.

Herzfeld, Hans. *Das Problem des deutschen Heeres 1919-1945.* Laupheim, Württemberg, 1954.

Höss, Rudolf. *Kommandant in Auschwitz. Autobiographische Aufzeichnungen. Kommentiert von Martin Broszat.* Stuttgart, 1958.

Hofer, Walther. *Der Nationalsozialismus. Dokumente 1933-1945* (Fischer-Bücherei, Bd. 172.) Frankfurt, 1957.

Hofer, Walther. *Die Entfesselung des zweiten Weltkrieges. Eine Studie über die internationalen Beziehungen im Sommer 1939.* Stuttgart, 1954.

Jetzinger, Franz. *Hitlers Jugend. Phantasien, Lügen und die Wahrheit.* Vienna, 1956.

Jong, Louis de. *Die deutsche fünfte Kolonne im zweiten Weltkrieg.* Stuttgart, 1958.

Klönne, Arno. *Hitlerjugend—Die Jugend und ihre Organisation im Dritten Reich.* Hanover/Frankfurt, 1955.

Kogon, Eugen. *Der SS-Staat. Das System der deutschen Konzentrationslager.* Düsseldorf, 1946.

Krausnick, Helmut. "Vorgeschichte und Beginn des militärischen Widerstands gegen Hitler". In "Aussenpolitik und Zeitgeschehen", Beilage zu *Das Parlament,* 1954, pp. 609-626.

(Krebs, Albert). *Tendenzen und Gestalten der NSDAP: Erinnerungen von Albert Krebs an die Frühzeit der NSDAP.* Stuttgart, 1959.

Kruck, Alfred. *Geschichte des Alldeutschen Verbandes.* Wiesbaden, 1954.

Mann, Golo. *Deutsche Geschichte im 19. und 20. Jahrhundert.* Frankfurt, 1958.

Mau, Hermann, and Helmut Krausnick. *Deutsche Geschichte der jüngsten Vergangenheit, 1933-1945.* Tübingen, Stuttgart, 1956.

Mohler, Armin. *Die Konservative Revolution in Deutschland 1918 bis 1932.* Stuttgart, 1950

Neurohr, Jean F. *Der Mythos vom Dritten Reich. Zur Geistesgeschichte des Nationalsozialismus.* Stuttgart, 1957.

Neusüss-Hunkel, Ermenhild. *Die SS.* Hanover, Frankfurt, 1956.

Niekisch, Ernst. *Das Reich der niederen Dämonen.* Hamburg, 1953.

Plessner, Helmut. *Die verspätete Nation. Über die politische Verführbarkeit bürgerlichen Geistes.* Stuttgart, 1959.

Reichmann, Eva G. *Flucht in den Hass. Die Ursachen der deutschen Judenkatastrophe.* Frankfurt, 1956.

Reitlinger, Gerald. *Die Endlösung. Hitlers Versuch der Ausrottung der Juden Europas 1939-1945.* Berlin, 1956.

Reitlinger, Gerald. *Die SS. Tragödie einer deutschen Epoche.* Vienna, Munich, Basel, 1957.

Ritter, Gerhard. *Carl Goerdeler und die deutsche Widerstandsbewegung.* Stuttgart, 1956.

Rothfels, Hans. *Die deutsche Opposition gegen Hitler* (Fischer-Bücherei, Bd. 198.). Frankfurt, 1958.

Schumann, Hans Gerd. *Nationalsozialismus und Gewerkschaftsbewegung. Die Vernichtung der deutschen Gewerkschaften und der Aufbau der Deutschen Arbeitsfront.* Hanover, Frankfurt, 1958.

Trevor-Roper, H. R. *Hitlers letzte Tage.* Zurich, 1948.

Tippelskirch, Kurt von. *Geschichte des 2. Weltkrieges.* 2nd ed., Bonn, 1956.

Volz, Hans. *Daten der Geschichte der NSDAP.* 6th ed., Berlin, Leipzig, 1936.

Wilmot, Chester. *Der Kampf um Europa.* 2nd ed., Frankfurt, 1954.

Biographic Dictionary and Index

The pages are indicated at the end of each biographic sketch. Dates and biographic information are given as of 1960, the year of publication of Broszat's original German work.

AMANN, Max (1891-1957). Hitler's sergeant during World War I. In 1921 he became the first business manager of the NSDAP and after 1922 the director of the Eher Verlag, the official Nazi publishing house. He was appointed the Party's Reich Leader for the Press. In 1933 he was made president of the Reich Press Chamber. (50)

ARNDT, Ernst Moritz (1796-1860). Historian and writer. During the struggle against Napoleon and for national unity Arndt was the most influential publicist of his day. Wrote pamphlets, patriotic songs, and other writings, in which he contrasted German character with that of the hated French and of the spirit of the French Revolution. He generated a feeling of national self-consciousness among the German people during the first half of the 19th century. (32)

BARTELS, Adolf (1862-1945). Professor and writer, author of numerous works on literary history *(Geschichte der Deutschen Literatur,* 2 vols., 1902), historical novels (D*ie Dithmarscher,* 1898), dramas, and poetic works with a strong folkish and *völkisch* character. He associated literary criticism with an uncompromising anti-Semitism, especially in his periodical *Deutsches Schrifttum* (1919-) and in a number of monographs (*Lessing und die Juden,*1918; *Die Berechtigung des Antisemitismus*). Bartels identified himself very early with National Socialism (*Der Nationalsozialismus Deutschlands Rettung,* 1924), but receded into the background after 1933. (34)

BÄUMLER, Alfred (1887-). Professor of Philosophy and Pedagogy at the Technical University, Dresden, 1929; appointed to the newly established chair of Political· Pedagogy at the University of Berlin, 1933. His writings *(Nietzsche der Philosoph und Politiker,* 1931; *Männerbund und Wissenschaft,*1934; *Politik und Erziehung,* 1937; *Alfred Rosenberg und der Mythos des 20. Jahrhunderts,* 1943; and others) placed him among the foremost academic apologists for National Socialism. In 1942 he was appointed Director of the ''Learned Subjects'' Division in Rosenberg's Organization for the Supervision of the Total Intellectual and Ideological Training and Education of the NSDAP. (33)

BENN, Gottfried (1886-1956). The most important lyricist and essayist of German expressionism. After taking a favorable position on the Third Reich *(Der neue Staat und die Intellektuellen,* 1933), he soon turned completely away from it and engaged in sharp criticism of the Third Reich. He reached the height of his poetic career after 1945. (18)

BISMARCK, Prince Otto von (1815-1898). After 1862 Prussian Minister President and Foreign Minister; Chancellor of the North German Federation, 1866; Chancellor of the German Empire, 1871-1890. (33)

BLANK, Herbert (Pseudonyms: Karsthans, Weigand v. Miltenberg) (ca. 1900-1959). Political journalist. Entered the NSDAP in 1925. Feuilletonist for Otto Strasser's *Berliner Arbeiter Zeitung,* collaborator on the *Nationalsozialistische Briefe,* and one of the founders of the *Schwarze Front* (1930). Placed in jail temporarily in 1933. Teacher at the Potsdam War Academy, 1934-1935; again arrested in 1935, after which he remained in a concentration camp until 1945. For a short period after 1945 he was the director of the North-West German Radio. Among his publications: *Soldaten; Adolf Hitler Wilhelm III.,* 1931; *Weichensteller Mensch. Ideen und Männer der Geschichte,* 1932; *Schleicher, Hitler?-Cromwell! Der Rhytmus der Geschichte,* 1932. (79)

BORMANN, Martin (1900-1945 ?) Member of the Free Corps Rossbach, 1919-1922; after 1933 Chief of Staff of the Führer's Deputy (Rudolf Hess) and Reich Leader of the NSDAP. From May 1941, Director of the Party Chancellery, Reich Minister and member of the Minister's Council for Defense. He was at the Führer's headquarters and exercised an increasingly commanding position in the final years. Reportedly killed after May 1, 1945, during the Battle of Berlin. (29, 50)

BRUCKER, Ludwig (1888-). Chairman of the Social-Political Committee of the Reich Directorate of the National Socialist Factory Cells Organization (NSBO), 1931. Director of the Department for Social Insurance in the German Labor Front (DAF), 1933-1934; deputy of Schuhmann in the Association of German Workers. Lost his position during the summer of 1934 because of differences with Ley. (84)

BRÜNING, Heinrich (1885-). One of the leading personalities in the Christian unions after 1920 and, since 1929, in the Center Party (*Zentrum*). Chancellor, 1930-1932. Emigrated to the USA in 1933. (77)

BUCHRUCKER, Bruno Ernst (1878-). Former major and leader in the Free Corps, organizer of the Black Reichswehr. He was condemned to several years imprisonment for his attempted Putsch in Küstrin in 1923. Joined the NSDAP in 1929; one of the founders of Otto Strasser's Black Front in 1930, arrested in 1933. Joined the Reichswehr in 1934. (79)

CHAMBERLAIN, Houston Stewart (1835-1927). British writer and cultural philosopher. After 1885 he became a German by choice and took up residence in Germany. He was a Wagner enthusiast and an admirer of the German spirit, of which he expected the salvation of the world. His writings, especially *Die Grundlagen des 19. Jahrhunderts*, 1899, with its glorification of Aryan creativity, strongly influenced National Socialist ideology (such as Rosenberg's). (33)

DAHN, Felix (1834-1912). Historical writer and the author of popular historical novels (*Ein Kampf um Rom*, 4 vols., 1876-78) and ballads. He spread an unscholarly but heroic image of the prehistoric *Völkerwanderung*, and of the early days of the Germanic tribes. (33)

DARRÉ, Richard Walter (1895-1953). Graduate agronomist, specialist in animal husbandry. Advocated an agrarian ideology based on racist theories (*Das Bauerntum als Lebensquell nordischer Rasse*, 1928). Joined the NSDAP in 1930 and was appointed to organize the peasants. Director of the Department of Agrarian Policies in the Party's Political Organization. During 1931-1938 he was chief of the SS Main Office for Race and Settlement with the rank of SS Lieutenant General. In 1933 he also became Reich Peasant Leader and Reich Minister of Food and Agriculture, a position he held until 1942. Among his many ideological writings are the following: *Neuadel aus Blut und Boden*, 1933; *Im Kampf um die Seele des deutschen Bauern*, 1934. He was the editor of the *Nationalsozialistische Landpost* and of the *Deutsche Agrarpost*. (38)

DINTER, Artur (1876-). Teacher, writer, and a member of the NSDAP since 1919. Deputy for the NSDAP in the Thuringian *Landtag*, from 1924. During 1925-1927 he was Gauleiter of the NSDAP in Thuringia. (46, 49)

DREXLER, Anton. Locksmith in Munich. He founded the *Freien Arbeitsausschuss für einen gerechten Frieden* (Free Working Committee for a Just Peace) in 1918, from which developed the *Deutsche Arbeiterpartei* (German Workers' Party), which became the NSDAP in 1920. During 1921-1923 he was honorary president of the NSDAP. He parted company with Hitler in 1925. He then founded the *Nationalsozialistische Volksbund* (National Socialist People's League). (20)

DÜHRING, Karl Eugen (1833-1921). Philosopher and economist. As a positivist and critic of society, Dühring carried on a passionate battle against Christianity and Judaism as well as against liberalism and Marxism. One of the first significant anti-Semites who based his anti-Semitism on racist theories *(Die Judenfrage als Rassen-, Sitten- und Kulturfrage,* 1881). (33, 36)

ECKEHART (also Eckart, Eckhart), Johannes (ca. 1260-1327). A Dominican—one of the most important German mystics and the creator of a religious-philosophical and metaphysical terminology in German. Rejected by the Church as a heretic, Eckehart was "rediscovered" by the idealists in German philosophy (Fichte, Schelling, Hegel) after a long period of oblivion. His name was used by those who propagated an "inward" German religiosity free of dogma. (33)

ECKART, Dietrich (1868-1923). Journalist, member of the Munich Thule Society and center of a *völkisch* circle. Joined the National Socialist movement in 1919 and supported it financially. First editor-in-chief of the *Völkischer Beobachter* (1921-1923). Participated in the 1923 Beer Hall Putsch. (36)

ESSER, Hermann (1900-). Founding member of the NSDAP, 1919; editor of the *Völkischer Beobachter* 1920, and until 1923, the leading agitator of the NSDAP aside from Hitler. Propaganda chief of the NSDAP, 1923-1925. Member of the Bavarian government since 1933, and from 1935 employed in the Reich Ministry for Propaganda. (72ff.)

FEDER, Gottfried (1883-1941). Founding member of the NSDAP. From 1924 member of the Reichstag and the *Reichsleitung* of the NSDAP. He developed the program of the NSDAP. Chairman of the Economic Council of the NSDAP, 1931; Undersecretary, later Reich Commissioner for Resettlement (Colonization), and professor at the Technical University in Berlin, 1933-1934. (21ff., 36, 48, 73)

FICHTE, Johann Gottlieb (1762-1814). Philosopher and political writer. As one of the last defenders of a rigorous state absolutism and state socialism *(Der geschlossene Handelsstaat,* 1800), and in the fight against Napoleon *(Der Patriotismus und sein Gegenteil,* 1807; *Reden an die Deutsche Nation,* 1807-1808), he was the herald of a missionary feeling for German nationalism. (32)

FORSTHOFF, Heinrich (1871-). Pastor, co-founder of the *Deutsch-Nationale Volkspartei*(German Nationalist People's Party or German Nationalist Party, DNVP) in 1919. After 1934 deputy state pastor in the Rhineland. Wrote, among other works, *Das Ende der humanistischen Illusion,*1933. (12)

FRANK, Hans (1900-1946). Director of the NSDAP's legal department. For a short while Minister of Justice in Bavaria, 1933. From 1934 Reich Minister without Portfolio, Reich Juridical Leader, and President of the Academy for German Law. Governor General of Poland 1939-1945. Executed in Nuremberg in 1946. (16, 21, 25ff., 36, 80)

FRAUENDORFER, Max (1909-). Staff member of the Party's Political Organization, 1931. Educational Director for the NSDAP, 1934; SS Lieutenant Colonel, Director-in-Chief of the Labor Department for the Governor General of Poland in Cracow, 1939-1942. Attempted to make contact with the resistance. Transferred to the army in 1942. (85)

FREISLER, Roland (1893-1945). World War I prisoner in Russia. After 1917 Bolshevik commissar; lawyer in Kassel, 1923; City Councillor for the *völkisch*-social bloc. Joined the NSDAP in 1925 and became a member of the Prussian *Landtag* in 1932. State Secretary in the Prussian Ministry of Justice, 1933, and after 1934 in the Reich Ministry of Justice. President of the People's Court, 1942-1945. Killed during an air raid on Berlin. (27)

FRICK, Wilhelm (1877-1946). Bavarian civil servant since 1904. Served in the Munich police headquarters and became a follower and supporter of Hitler, 1922-1923. Imprisoned after the Hitler Putsch in 1923. Reichstag deputy, 1924; Minister of People's Education in Thuringia, 1930; from 1933 until 1943 Minister of the Interior. Executed in Nuremberg in 1946. (38, 76)

FRITSCH, Theodor Emil (1852-1933). Writer and publisher. Toward the end of the 19th century he founded an association of the middle class in Saxony. Author of numerous anti-Semitic publications, especially the *Antisemiten-Katechismus*, which appeared for the first time in 1887 and was thereafter frequently reprinted, and of the *Handbuch der Judenfrage*, 1907. He was also the editor of the anti-Semitic periodical *Der Hammer*, founder and owner of the *völkisch* anti-Semitic Hammer publishing house in Leipzig, and organizer of the Hammer Societies and of the Reich Hammer League. He was one of the most active anti-Semites of the Imperial period and was celebrated by the National Socialists as the "Old Master" of their ideology. (34, 36)

GLAGAU, Otto. Catholic publicist, who took a position against liberalism and against emancipated urban

Jewry during the 1870's and 1880's, in such magazines as *Germania* and the *Gartenlaube,* as well as in his own brochures. His writings include *Der Börsen und Gründungsschwindel in Berlin,* 1876, and *Des Reiches Not und der neue Kulturkampf,* 1879. (36)

GOBINEAU, Count Joseph Arthur (1816-1882). French diplomat and writer, a student of Auguste Comte. His most influential work,*The Inequality of Human Races,* 1853-1855, was the first attempt at a historical philosophy based on racist theories in which the Aryans figured as an elite race. Gobineau's teaching fell on fertile soil in Germany. He counted among his adherents such men as Nietzsche, Wagner and Chamberlain. (32)

GOEBBELS, Joseph (1897-1945). Manager of the Ruhr area for the NSDAP, 1925-1926, and editor of the *Nationalsozialistische Briefe;* Gauleiter in Berlin, 1926; publisher of the newspaper *Angriff;* Reich Propaganda Chief for the NSDAP, 1930; Reich Minister of Public Enlightenment and Propaganda, 1933. He died by suicide in 1945. (25, 27, 50, 59, 61, 65, 75, 80, 87)

GÖRING, Hermann (1893-1946). During World War I he was the last commanding officer of the Richthofen fighter squadron. In 1923 he became the first leader of the SA and went to Berlin in 1927 as Hitler's personal representative. President of the Reichstag, 1932; Minister President of Prussia, 1933; Aviation Minister and Commander-in-Chief of the Air Force,

1935; Reich Marshal and successor-designate of Hitler, 1940. Died by suicide in Nuremberg Prison in 1946. (50)

GÖRZ, Count. Director of the Leader Circle of *völkisch* fighting organizations in Thuringia during the 1920's. He did not play a prominent role thereafter. (46)

GRAEFE, Albrecht von (1868-1933). Landowner and former officer; member of the German Nationalist Party, founder of the *Deutsch-Völkische Freiheitspartei* (German-*Völkisch* Freedom Party) in 1922. (45, 55)

GRASSMANN, Peter (1873-). Chairman of the Association of German Printers, 1908-1919; Deputy Chairman of the German Federation of Trade Unions, 1919-1933; Reichstag deputy, 1924; temporarily imprisoned during 1933. (82)

GÜNTHER, Albrecht Erich (1893-). Editor and co-publisher of the journal *Deutsches Volkstum*. Among his other works are: *Totem: Tier und Mensch im Lebenszusammenhang*, 1927; *Geist der Jungmannschaft*, 1934. (12)

GÜNTHER, Hans F. K. (1891-). Anthropologist and political publicist. His numerous works on race (*Rassenkunde des deutschen Volkes*, 1922: *Rassenkunde Europas*, 1924; *Der nordische Gedanke und die Deutschen*, 1927; *Herkunft und Rassengeschichte der*

Germanen, 1934, and many others), which mixed scientific insights with a hero-building mystical ideology, were extremely helpful to National Socialism. (38)

GÜRTNER, Franz (1881-1941). Member of the German National Party. During the Hitler Putsch and the trial he was Bavarian Minister of Justice, 1923-1924; Reich Minister of Justice, 1932-1941. (27)

HABERMANN, Max (1885-1944). From 1918 to 1933 a leading member of the boards of the German National Clerks Association, of the German Federation of Trade Unions and of the International League of Christian Unions. He was a confidant of Brüning and participated, during 1930-1932, in the attempts to find a means of co-operating with the Strasser wing of the NSDAP. He had some hopes for National Socialism but later turned away from it and toward the resistance groups among the former unions, led by Jakob Kaiser and Wilhelm Leuschner. He was arrested after the attempt on Hitler's life on July 20, 1944, and committed suicide in prison. (17)

HAUG, Richard, and Eugen HAUG. Founders and influential members of *völkisch* anti-Semitic groups in Stuttgart since the 1890's. They participated in the creation of the Stuttgart group of the NSDAP, but later were not prominent in politics. (36)

HEGEL, Georg Wilhelm Friedrich (1770-1831). Philosopher. His basic concepts on the philosophy of the state, law, and history played a decisive part in all subsequent German philosophy, political science, and history. He influenced Marx deeply. Hegel's ideas were also used falsely by the Fascists and the Nazis as the theoretical justification for their deification of the state. (33)

HELD, Heinrich (1868-1938). Member of the Bavarian Landtag (Center Party) since 1907; one of the founders of the Bavarian People's Party in 1918 and the leader of its faction in the Bavarian Landtag from 1919 until 1924; Minister President of Bavaria, 1924-1933. (48)

HERDER, Johann Gottfried (1744-1803). Philosopher and poet. As a cultural historian, publisher of folk poetry, and translator, Herder acted as the cosmopolitan transmitter of foreign culture. In contrast to the rationalism of his time he emphasized the natural folk source of literature and culture. He is regarded in Germany and among the Slavic peoples, frequently in error, as a progenitor of a chauvinistic nationalism. (32)

HESS, Rudolf (1894-). Member of the NSDAP from 1920; participated in the 1923 Hitler Putsch. Student of the geopolitician Karl Haushofer in Munich. Hitler's private secretary, 1925-1932; Hitler's deputy from 1933, and Reich Minister. On his own initiative flew to Great Britain in 1941 to arrange a settlement between the two countries. Condemned to life imprisonment at Nuremberg in 1946. (84)

HEYDRICH, Reinhard (1904-1942). Lost his commission in the navy by decision of a court of honor in 1931; Chief of the SS Security Service (SD), 1932; as Himmler's right hand he incorporated the police departments of the various Länder into a national force, 1933-1934; in 1939 appointed head of the Central Security Office which included the Gestapo, Criminal Investigation Department, and the Security Service for all of Germany; assassinated by Czech resistance organization in 1942 while serving as Acting Reich Protector of Bohemia and Moravia. (29)

HIELSCHER, Friedrich (1902-). Political writer. Before 1933 he belonged to the Ernst Jünger circle of the "new nationalism". During the Third Reich he deliberately entered service on Himmler's staff in order to prepare resistance measures from inside. Not politically active since 1945. Major works: *Das Reich*, 1931; *Fünfzig Jahre unter Deutschen*, 1954. (17)

HIMMLER, Heinrich (1900-1945). Secretary to Gregor Strasser, 1925-1927; Reich Leader of the SS, 1929; Chief of the Political Police in Bavaria and all other German Länder, 1933-1934; Chief of the German Police, 1936; from 1939 Reich Commissar for the Strengthening of the German Nation; Reich Minister for the Interior, 1943; Commander of the Reserve

Army, 1944. Committed suicide after arrest by the British in 1945. (25, 27, 52)

HITLER, Adolf (1889-1945). Member of the NSDAP from 1919, chairman from 1921; changed title to *Führer* (Leader) in 1925. From 1933 Führer and Reich Chancellor, and after the death of President Hindenburg, on August 8, 1934, took over the powers of the presidency. Committed suicide on April 30, 1945 in Berlin. (passim)

HUGENBERG, Alfred (1865-1951). One of the founders of the All-German Association, 1890; member of the Reichstag, 1920; chairman of the German Nationalist Party, 1928; controlled a large number of German newspapers (Scherl Verlag; Vera Verlagsanstalt; Ala-Anzeigen AG; Telegraphenunion) as well as the Universum-Film AG (UFA) through the *Wirtschaftsvereinigung*, founded in 1919. In 1929 he co-operated with the NSDAP in the agitation against the Young Plan and in 1931 formed the Harzburger Front with Hitler. He was Minister of Economics in Hitler's cabinet until June 1933. (23, 77)

JAHN, Friedrich Ludwig (1778-1852). *Turnvater*, originator of gymnastics as a special form of physical education. He contributed toward nationalism during the French occupation of Prussia and during the Restoration. He was influential because of his lectures on German nationality in 1817-1818. The popularity which Jahn's courage brought him extended to his writings (*Deutsche Turnkunst,* 1816; *Deutsches Volkstum,* 1819; and others) and, undeservedly, to his amateurish intellectual and political activities. (32)

JOHST, Hanns (1890-). Writer and dramatist. Producer at the Prussian State Theater, 1933, and president of the Academy for German Poetry; head of the Reich Chamber for Literature. He used his influence in the creation of a new theater in the spirit of National Socialism. (12)

JUNG, Edgar (1894-1934). Lawyer and political writer. He belonged to the circle of the Young Conservatives and the German Club which developed from the June Club in 1926. From 1932 he was von Papen's confidant and primarily responsible for the latter's spectacular protest speech against the Nazis at Marburg (June 17, 1934). Because of it he was arrested and shot on Göring's personal order during the terror actions of the Röhm affair (June 30, 1934). (16)

JÜNGER, Ernst (1895-) Poet and political writer. His influence after World War I rested primarily on his war books (*In Stahlgewittern,* 1920; *Der Kampf als inneres Erlebnis,* 1922; and others), and on his book, *Der Arbeiter,* 1932, as well as on essays published in various magazines. These preached "heroic realism" and the "new nationalism". He avoided linking himself with the NSDAP and his novels developed covert criticism of Hitler and the Third Reich (*Marmorklippen,* 1939). (17)

JÜNGER, Friedrich Georg (1898-). Political writer and poet. Like his brother Ernst he was an advocate of radical nationalist activism before 1933. After 1933 he did not play a political role. Since 1945 he has achieved extensive recognition as a lyrical poet and cultural critic. (17)

KASCHE, Siegfried (1903-1947). Participated in the Baltic fighting against the Bolsheviks; member of the German *Völkisch* Freedom Party, joined the NSDAP in 1926; became Deputy Gauleiter and SA Major General in the Ostmark (Lausitz); lost his position after the Röhm affair. German Minister in Zagreb, 1941-1944. He was executed in Yugoslavia in 1947. (60)

KELLERMANN, H.   Publishing House Alexander Duncker (Weimar). Founder and leader of the Association of *Völkisch* Publishers, Leipzig, 1920. (34)

KOSSINNA, Gustaf (1858-1931). Scholar in pre-history, professor at the University of Berlin, 1902-1927. Major works: *Die deutsche Vorgeschichte eine hervorragend nationale Wissenschaft*, 1912; *Die Indogermanen*, 1921; *Ursprung und Verbreitung der Germanen in vor- und frühgeschichtlicher Zeit*, 1928; *Altgermanische Kulturhöhe*, 1927. Founder of the Society for German Pre-history and publisher of the journal *Mannus* since 1909. (36)

KRAUS, Karl (1874-1936). Writer, satirist and language critic. Editor of *Fackel* since 1899. His social criticism took the form of satire of impure language. His posthumously published criticism of National Socialism, *Die Dritte Walpurgisnacht*, is a masterwork of such satirical unmasking. (38)

KRÜGER, O. E. Member of the National Socialist Factory Cells Organization (NSBO); collaborator on the NSBO journal *Der Betrieb*, 1933. He was removed, together with other leftist NSBO people during the summer of 1934. (84)

LAGARDE, Paul Anton de (1827-1891). Orientalist, philologist, and political writer. When criticizing the materialism of his time, Lagarde demanded the care and intensification of German ways and morals as the source of moral cleansing and of a new religion. His *Deutsche Schriften* (2 vols., 1878-1881) served, especially after 1918, as the justification of an absolute *völkisch* nationalism and exercised a great influence. (33, 36)

LANGBEHN, Julius (1851-1907). Author of the sensational *Rembrandt als Erzieher* which appeared anonymously in 1890. It contained a severe and influential criticism of one-sided intellectual education, and posited the natural and poetic development of the individual as the ideal aim of German education. Langbehn thus set the direction for an emphatic cultural conservatism as well as the movement of folk art. (33)

LANGE, Friedrich (1852-1917). Political writer. Founder of the anti-Semitic *Deutschbund* in 1894. Its constitution and ideology were presented in Lange's work *Reines Deutschtum.* In 1895 he founded the *Deutsche Zeitung* (Berlin) as the newspaper of all-German *völkisch* persuasion, which continued its existence into the Weimar period. (34)

LEIPART, Theodor (1867-1947). Chairman of the Woodworkers Organization in the Free Unions, 1908; President of the Free Unions, 1920; temporarily arrested in 1933. (82)

LEY, Robert (1890-1945). Gauleiter of the NSDAP in the Rhineland; Reich Political Organization Leader of the German Labor Front (DAF), 1933. Committed suicide in prison in Nuremberg in 1945. (81, 84)

LIEBENFELS, Jörg Lanz von (also Jörg or Josef Lanz) (1874-1954). Assumed his aristocratic title on his own authority; novice in the Heiligenkreuz monastery. Starting with a new interpretation of the Knights Templar, Lanz developed an ideology which dealt with the historical battle between the blond heroes (the Aryan heroes) and the "low-life, nasty" mixed races. He left the monastery in 1899 and founded the Order of the New Temple *(Ordensburg Werfenstein).* He published the journal *Ostara* (1905-1931), and advanced a creed of racial purity. He used the swastika flag as a symbol and later considered himself the father of National Socialism. In 1938 Hitler prohibited further publication of his works. (38)

LUDENDORFF, Erich von (1868-1937). During World War I he was Quartermaster General in the Supreme

Command of the Army under Hindenburg and, from
1916, the strategist of the war effort and of the policies
determining the conduct of the war. He participated
in the Hitler Putsch in 1923; together with Gregor
Strasser and von Graefe he headed the National
Socialist Freedom Party (*Nationalsozialistische Frei-
heitspartei*), 1924-1925. In 1925 he broke with Hitler.
With his wife Mathilde, he founded the Fighting
Organization Against Supra-National Powers and the
Tannenberg League (German-Germanic Religious
Community). (45, 48, 60)

MAHRAUN, Artur (1890-1950). Founder of the Order
of Young Germans, 1920. He was one of the founders
of the State Party, 1932, and as such a strong opponent
of the NSDAP; he was briefly imprisoned in 1933. (62)

MANN, Thomas (1875-1955). One of Germany's greatest writers. Member of the Academy for German
Language and Poetry in Berlin. Emigrated to Switzerland in 1933, later to USA. His German citizenship
was revoked by the Nazi government. (40ff., 54)

MOELLER van den BRUCK, Arthur (1876-1925). One
of the founders of the June Club in Berlin and its
intellectual pivot, 1915-1925. The June Club had a
lasting influence on the young conservative movement.
Most important political writings: *Der preussische
Stil*, 1916; *Das Recht der jungen Völker*, 1919; *Das
Dritte Reich*, 1923. Committed suicide in 1925. (17,
40, 72)

MOSSAKOWSKY, Eugen (1897-). Journalist. For a time he was a member of the Saxon Old Socialists (like Niekisch and Winnig); collaborator for the Strasser publications *Nationalsozialistische Briefe* and *Der Nationale Sozialist,* 1927; manager of the Reichstag faction of the NSDAP, 1928-1930; founder, with Otto Strasser, of the Black Front, 1920; temporarily arrested in 1933; later detailed to Army counterintelligence *(Abwehr).* (79)

MUCHOW, Reinhold (1905-1933). Joined the NSDAP in 1925; organizational chief of the Gau Berlin, 1928; organizer of the National Socialist Factory Cells Organization (NSBO), 1930-1933; played a decisive role in the measures taken against the independent unions on May 2, 1933; chief of the organization bureau of the German Labor Front; killed in an accident on September 12, 1933. (66ff., 82ff.)

MUTSCHMANN, Martin (1879-1945). Gauleiter of the NSDAP in Saxony from 1925; *Reichsstatthalter* (governor) of Saxony, 1933-1945. He died in 1945 while imprisoned by the USSR. (81)

MUSSOLINI, Benito (1883-1945). Socialist party politician and journalist, 1902-1914; founder of the Italian Fascist Party, 1919; seized power by a coup d'état (March on Rome), 1922; arrested in 1943 by the royalist opposition led by Marshal Badoglio, but liberated by German parachute troops; shot by Italian partisans in Northern Italy in 1945. (47, 49, 59)

NAUMANN, Friedrich (1860-1919) Evangelical theologian and politician, liberal speaker for the Christian-Social movement during the Empire; in 1896 founder of the National Social Association which aimed at the reconciliation of the workers with the imperial Germany (*Demokratie und Kaisertum,* 1900); as the editor of the periodical *Hilfe,* since 1895, he was the focus for enlightened liberalism. One of the founders of the Democratic Party in 1918 and collaborator in the drafting of the Weimar Constitution. (71)

NIEKISCH, Ernst (1889-). Politician and political writer. Chairman of the Council of the Bavarian Soviet Republic in 1919; leader of the Bavarian Independent Socialists (USPD); editor of *Widerstand,* 1926-1934, and as such one of the main representatives of national bolshevism; arrested in 1937 and condemned to life imprisonment by the People's Court in 1939. He joined the SED (Socialist Unity Party, i.e. Communist Party in East Germany) in 1945 and separated from it in 1948. (72, 84)

NIETZSCHE, Friedrich (1844-1900). Philosopher. His concept of the master ethic and his work *Wille zur Macht* were misconstrued in the most primitive way by his *völkisch* and National Socialist interpreters, and were misused to bolster race theories. (33)

PAPEN, Franz von (1879-). Represented the right wing of the Center Party in the Prussian *Landtag,* 1920-1932; Chancellor and Reich Commissar for Prussia, 1932; Vice-Chancellor, 1933-1934; from

1936, ambassador in Vienna and Ankara; acquitted at the Nuremberg Trials in 1946. (27)

PFEFFER von SALOMON, Fritz (1892-). Army Captain (retired). Highest SA Leader, 1927-1930; SA Major General and Chief of Police in Kassel, 1933; arrested in connection with the attempted assassination of Hitler on July 20, 1944. Active in the German Party (*Deutsche Partei*) of Hesse after 1945. (77)

RAUSCHNING, Hermann (1887-). Until 1926 he was active in German organizations in Poland; moved to Danzig Free State; landowner; joined the NSDAP and became chairman of the Danzig State Association (*Landbund*); president of the Danzig Senate, 1933-1934; emigrated to Switzerland in 1936 and later to the USA. Rauschning was a very effective publicist against Nazism because of his revelations (*Gespräche mit Hitler*) and his penetrating analyses of National Social-ism (*Revolution des Nihilismus*, etc.). (38)

RENTELN, Theodor Adrian von (1897-). Studied political science and economics in Berlin; Reich Leader of the Hitler Youth, 1931-1932; member of the political-economic department of the Reich direc-torate of the NSDAP, 1932-1933; leader of the National Socialist Fighting Organization of the middle class trades (*NS-Hago*); Commissar General of Lithuania in World War II. (85)

REUPKE, Hans (1892-). Lawyer. Member of the administration of the Reich Association of German

Industry, 1927; joined the NSDAP in 1930. Writings: *Das Wirtschaftssystem des Faschismus*, 1932; *Unternehmer und Arbeiter in der Faschistischen Wirtschaftsidee*, 1931. (23)

REVENTLOW, Count Ernst (1869-1943). Naval officer until 1899; writer, editor of *Reichswart* from 1920. One of the founders of the German *Völkisch* Freedom Party. Reichstag deputy of the NSDAP from 1928. (48)

RIBBENTROP, Joachim von (1893-1946). Plenipotentiary Extraordinary on special mission (*Dienststelle Ribbentrop*), 1935; ambassador to London, 1936; Foreign Minister, 1938-1945. Executed at Nuremberg in 1946. (24)

RÖHM, Ernst (1887-1934). Captain in the Reichswehr, adjutant of General von Epp, commanding in Munich; retired from the army in 1923 and participated in the Hitler Putsch; separated from Hitler in 1925 and served in the Bolivian army; Chief of Staff of the SA, 1931; Minister without Portfolio, 1933. Shot on Hitler's personal orders on June 30, 1934, during the so-called Röhm Putsch. (77, 80)

ROSENBERG, Alfred (1893-1946). Editor-in-chief of the *Völkischer Beobachter* from 1922. When the NSDAP was outlawed after the Beer Hall Putsch, Rosenberg, as Hitler's deputy, founded the Greater German People's Community; founder of the Fighting League for German Culture, 1929; editor of the *National-*

sozialistische Monatshefte from 1930. Chief of the
Department for Foreign Affairs of the NSDAP and
Plenipotentiary for the Total Ideological Training and
Education of the NSDAP, 1933-1934; Reich Minister
for the Occupied Eastern Territories, 1941-1945.
Executed at Nuremberg in 1946. (15, 21, 24ff., 33,
36, 49, 74)

ROTH, Alfred (pseudonym: Otto Arnim) (1879-ca.
1940). Writer and journalist. Propagandist for the
German National Association of Sales Clerks (DHV);
editor of the DHV organ, *Die Deutsche Handelswacht,*
until 1910; in his position as Manager of the German
Völkisch Protection and Defense League, of the Association of German *Völkisch* Leagues, Hamburg, and
organizer of the annual German Day, Roth was one
of the main organizers of German *Völkisch* endeavors.
After 1933, he was editor of the *Spirale (Hamburger
Beobachter)*. Among his writings: *So sah ich den
Krieg,* 1934; *Kampf ums Deutschtum,* 1936. (34)

SCHACHT, Hjalmar (1877-). Reich Commissar for
Currency and President of the Reichsbank, 1923-1930;
Reich Minister of Economics, 1934-1937; arrested in
1944; acquitted at the Nuremberg Trials. (23, 77)

SCHEMANN, Karl Ludwig (1852-). Race researcher
and historian who defended the racial theories of
Gobineau and translated his writings; founded the
Gobineau Association in 1894 and the Gobineau Mu-
seum in Strassburg in 1906. Among his writings:

Gobineaus Rassenwerk, 1910;   *Quellen und Untersu-
chungen zum Leben Gobineaus*,   2 vols., 1914-1920;
Rasse in den Geisteswissenschaften, 3 vols., 1928-
1931. (36)

SCHERINGER, Richard (1904-). Officer in the German
Army, 1924; became known because of the trial in
Ulm in 1930; joined the German Communist Party in
1931. (79ff.)

SCHMITT, Kurt (1886-). Director-General of the
Allianz-Versicherungs AG., 1921; Hitler's economic
advisor before 1933; Reich Minister of Economics in
1933-1934, after Hugenberg's resignation. (23)

SCHÖNERER, Georg Ritter von (1842-1921). Landowner and politician. Member of the Austrian Chamber
of Deputies and a supporter of the extreme German
Nationalists; author of the Pan-German Linz Program,
1882, and founder of the Austrian Pan-German Movement; major promoter of the anti-Catholic *Los von
Rom* movement. Editor of *Unverfälschte Worte*, 1890-
1912, of the *Alldeutsches Tageblatt* and the *Grazer
Wochenblatt*. Among his writings: *Zwölf Reden*, 1886;
Fünf Reden, 1891. (42)

SCHRÖDER, Baron Kurt von (1889-). Partner in the
banking house of I. H. Stein in Cologne, 1921; President
of the Chamber of Industry and Commerce in Cologne;
arranged the talk between von Papen and Hitler in

January 1933 which led the way to the formation of the Hitler cabinet. (77)

SCHUHMANN, Walter (1898-). Member of the Berlin City Council, 1929; Reichstag deputy of the NSDAP in 1930; leader of the Association of all Workers *(Gesamtverband)* in the German Labor Front, 1931. (84)

SOREL, Georges (1847-1922). French sociologist. His teachings about revolutionary action and violence, *Reflexions sur la violence*, had their influence not only on French proletarian syndicalism but also on the right-wing *Action française*. Mussolini was also influenced by Sorel, as was Lenin. (59)

SPANN, Othmar (1878-). Philosopher, economist, and sociologist. He confronted liberalism and Marxism with an economic and theoretical sociological "Universalism" which was connected with Catholic and conservative sociology and which emphasized the relation of the individual to class and nationality. Among his works: *Der wahre Staat*,   1921; *Gesellschafts-philosophie,* 1928. (85ff.)

SPENGLER, Oswald (1880-1936). Philosopher of history. Teacher in a *Gymnasium* (secondary school) in Hamburg, 1908-1911; free lance writer in Munich after 1911. His major work *The Decline of the West*, 2 vols., 1918-1922, became an international success.

However, Spengler's political influence is based on his smaller works such as *Preussentum und Sozialismus*, 1919; *Neubau des Deutschen Reiches*, 1924; *Politische Pflichten der deutschen Jugend*, 1924; *Politische Schriften*, 1932; *Reden und Aufsätze*, 1937. (13ff., 40, 72)

STAPEL, Wilhelm (1882-1954). Political writer. Manager of the Dürer League and editor of *Kunstwart*, 1911-1916; director of the Hamburg People's Home, 1917-1919; later free lance journalist in Hamburg; editor of the *Deutsches Volkstum*, 1919-1938. Among his writings: *Avenarius-Buch*, 1916; *Volksbürgerliche Erziehung*, 3rd edition, 1927; *Antisemitismus und Antigermanismus*, 1927; *Die Fiktion der Weimarer Verfassung*, 1927; *Die Kirche Christi und der Staat Hitlers*, 1933; *Volkskirche oder Sekte?*,1934; *Die literarische Vorherrschaft der Juden*,1937. (12)

STAUSS, Emil Georg von (1877-). Director of the *Deutsche Bank*; member of the German People's Party and member of the Reichstag from 1930. He got in touch with Hitler in 1932 and negotiated the financing of the NSDAP. (77)

STENNES, Walter (1897-). Police captain; after 1919 he transferred from the Black Reichswehr to the SA; highest SA leader in East Elbe area, 1929; removed from the SA by Hitler in 1932; arrested in 1933. Became military advisor to Chiang Kai-shek in 1934 and returned to Germany in 1949. (77)

STINNES, Hugo (1870-1924). Creator of the Stinnes industrial combine. Together with Thyssen and Kirdorf, he financed the NSDAP as early as 1923. (77)

STÖCKER, Adolf (1835-1909). Chaplain to the Imperial Court and pastor of the Cathedral in Berlin, 1874-1889. He combined the orthodox Protestantism of the national church with the attempt to win the workers for the state. He used popular anti-Semitism in the battle against liberalism, individualism, and materialism. The Christian-social movement which originated with him had primarily a middle class character and influenced, among others, the Protestant student organization (VDSt). (36, 72)

STRASSER, Gregor (1892-1934). First Lieutenant (retired), pharmacist. Provincial leader and SA Leader in Lower Bavaria, 1920; member of the Reich Directorate of the National Socialist Freedom Party, 1924; organizer of the NSDAP in North and West Germany, member of the Reichstag, 1925-1926; Reich Director for Propaganda, 1926-1932; Reich Leader for Organization of the NSDAP, 1932; broke with Hitler toward the end of 1932. Shot in 1934 in Berlin in connection with the Röhm purge. (23, 39, 45, 73ff., 79ff.)

STRASSER, Otto (1897-). Originally a social democrat. Participated actively in the fight against the Kapp Putsch in 1920; in 1924 joined the National Socialist Freedom Party and the NSDAP in 1925. Worked in the Nazi press in Berlin (Kampf-Verlag). Broke with

Hitler in 1930. Strasser founded the Fighting Union of
Revolutionary National Socialists (Black Front); emigrated in 1933 and returned to West Germany in 1955.
(73ff., 77ff.)

STREICHER, Julius (1885-1946). One of the founders
of the German Social Party *(Deutsch-Soziale Partei)*,
1919; organizer for the NSDAP in Nuremberg and its
surroundings, 1921; publisher of the anti-Semitic
smear newspaper *Der Stürmer*; Gauleiter of Franconia,
1925. Streicher was executed after the Nuremberg
Trials in 1946. (36, 73)

THYSSEN, Fritz (1873-1951). Chairman of the Board
of the United Steel Works, Düsseldorf; member of the
NSDAP and financial supporter of Hitler since 1923;
appointed Prussian State Councillor in 1933 and
charged with the preliminary work on the construction
of the corporative state; emigrated in 1938. (77, 85)

ULLMANN, Hermann (1884-1958). High school teacher. Editor of the *Kunstwart*, 1908-1912; editor of
Deutsche Arbeit, 1912; department chairman of the
Association for Germandom Abroad (VDA), 1918;
editor-in-chief of *Deutsche*, 1920-1923; editor of the
Politische Wochenschrift, 1924-1931; employed in the
directorate of the publishing house Scherl, 1926-1929;
one of the leaders of the VDA, 1933. Among his
writings are: *Das werdende Volk*, 1929; *Durchbruch
zur Nation. Geschichte des deutschen Volkes, 1929
bis 33*, 1933; *Das Südostdeutschtum*, 1935; *Das 19.*

Jahrhundert. Volk gegen Masse im Kampf um die Gestalt Europas, 1936. (17)

UNRUH, Friedrich Franz von (1893-). Captain (retired); free-lance writer since 1919; went into exile to USA during World War II. (63)

WILSER, Ludwig (1850-1923). Physician and race researcher. Author of popular writings on race history, among them *Die Herkunft der Deutschen,* 1885; *Stammbaum und Ausbreitung der Germanen,* 1895; *Germanischer Stil und deutsche Kunst,* 1899; *Herkunft und Urgeschichte der Arier,* 1899; *Die Germanen,* 1904. (36)

WINNIG, August (1878-1956). Politician and writer. Chairman of the German Construction Workers Association, 1913; Plenipotentiary for the Baltic Area and Reich Commissar for East and West Prussia, 1918; President of East Prussia, 1918. Expelled from the Social Democratic Party in 1920 because of his participation in the Kapp Putsch; member of the Old Socialists *(Altsozialisten),* 1927; joined the People's Conservatives in 1930. His departure from Marxism and adherence to a corporativist Christian ideal of a national community temporarily attracted him to Nazism, which tolerated his public activities and his work as a publicist. During World War II, Winnig had connections with various German resistance groups, but did not become an active participant.

Among his writings: *Vom Proletariat zum Arbeiter-
tum,* 1930; *Heimkehr,* 1935; *Aus 20 Jahren,* 1947.
(12, 16, 72)

WOLTMANN, Ludwig (1871-1907). Physician, journalist, and anthropologist. Supported the interpretation
of history based on Gobineau's race theories; founded
the *Politisch-Anthropologische Revue,* 1902; his major
work: *Politische Anthropologie,* 1903. (36)

WULLE, Reinhold (1882-). Director of the publishing
office of the *Deutsche Zeitung,* 1918-1921; Reichstag
deputy for the German Nationalist Party (DNVP); one
of the founders of the German *Völkisch* Freedom
Party, 1922; after 1933 temporarily kept in a concentration camp. (45)

Chronology:
The Rise and Fall
of German National Socialism

AND SOME OTHER HISTORICAL LANDMARKS

Prepared by Kurt Rosenbaum

1918

March
: Anton Drexler organizes the Independent Workers' Committee in Munich. This is a predecessor of the Nazi Party.

November 11
: Armistice. End of the First World War.

1919

January
: Formation of the German Workers' Party in Munich.

January 5-6	General strike and Communist uprising in Berlin.
January 19	Election for the Constituent Assembly, to form a new government.
February 6	Provisional government meets in Weimar.
April 4-May 1	Soviet Republic in Bavaria.
July 31	Germany adopts the Weimar Constitution.
September	Hitler joins the German Workers' Party as member No. 7.

1920

February	Twenty-five Points (Party program) adopted.
March 13-17	Kapp Putsch against the German government.
	Von Kahr government (Rightist) rules in Bavaria.
April	Hitler resigns from the army to devote himself fully to the development of the Party.

August	The German Workers' Party becomes the National Socialist German Workers' Party, *Nationalsozialistische Deutsche Arbeiterpartei* (NSDAP).
August 26	Erzberger, Minister of Finance, murdered by Rightist extremists.
December	Purchase of the newspaper *Völkischer Beobachter* which becomes the official newspaper of the Party.

1921

July	Hitler becomes chairman of the Nazi Party (NSDAP).
October	Organization of the *Sturmabteilung* (SA) for the purpose of guarding Nazi meetings and breaking up those of the opposition.

1922

June 24	Walther Rathenau, Foreign Minister, murdered by Rightist extremists. A law to protect the Republic is directed against all extremist groups, including the NSDAP.
June–July	Hitler imprisoned for violence against political opponents.

1923

Streicher, a rabid anti-Semite, begins the publication of the pornographic *Der Stürmer,* an anti-Semitic hatesheet.

January

Inflation begins to assume disastrous proportions ($1 equals 17,000 marks).

January 11

French and Belgian forces occupy the Ruhr industrial area. The German government proclaims passive resistance.

May 1

20,000 heavily armed SA men concentrate near Munich to smash May Day celebrations of the Communists and the Social Democrats. The army intervenes and Hitler calls off the attack.

September 26

End of passive resistance in the Ruhr area. The Kahr government declares a state of emergency in Bavaria. Kahr receives dictatorial powers to suppress extremism.

The Reich government declares a state of emergency and gives dictatorial powers to the Minister of

Defense, i.e. the Reichswehr. (Decree rescinded in February 1924).

October   The Reich government bans the Nazi
newspaper *Völkischer Beobachter*
for scurrilous attacks on leading
Germans and orders the arrest of
extremist leaders (Heiss, Ehrhardt,
Rossbach) domiciled in Bavaria. The
Bavarian government (Kahr) refuses
to co-operate with Berlin.

Communists legally enter the gov-
ernments of Thuringia and Saxony.
An uprising of the Communists in
Hamburg fails.

October 27   Kahr demands the resignation of the
Reich government and orders those
of the armed bands which support
him to concentrate on the borders of
Bavaria and Thuringia.

End of October   The Reichswehr removes Communists from the governments of Thur-
ingia and Saxony. An attempted Communist revolution is suppressed.

November 8   A mass meeting is called by Kahr
in the Munich Bürgerbräu Keller
and invaded by Hitler who proclaims

the start of the "national revolution." Kahr is forced to join a
"national government." During the
night Nazis seize the Munich Reichswehr headquarters; however, not a
single strategic position is secured.

November 9   Nazi Putsch fails. Two to three
thousand armed SA men led by Hit-
ler and General Ludendorff march
to the center of Munich. They are
stopped by about 100 policemen as
they enter the Odeonsplatz. The police open fire and the Nazi leaders,
including Hitler, flee. Ludendorff
and his aide are arrested and the
Nazi Party is outlawed in Germany.

November 11   Hitler is arrested and held in cus-
tody in the Landsberg fortress.

November 15   Inflation is ended by the introduction
of the *Rentenmark*.

1924-1929 Years of Economic Stability in Germany.

1924

February 26   The treason trial opens, with Hitler
and Ludendorff as the main defen-
dants. Hitler turns the proceedings

into a propaganda victory for his cause.

March 22
Ludendorff is acquitted. Hitler receives the minimum sentence of five years.

May 4
Reichstag elections. Communists and Right extremists gain. The Nazis and the *völkisch* groups receive 1,918,300 votes, 6.5% of the total votes cast, entitling them for the first time to seats in the Reichstag: 32 in the 472-member Reichstag.

December 7
Reichstag elections. Popular vote of the Nazis goes down to 907,300, 3.0% of the total votes cast. Their number of seats drops to 14 of the 493-member Reichstag.

December 20
Hitler is released after having been imprisoned for nine months. During this time he completed the draft of volume 1 of *Mein Kampf*.

1925
February 24
Refounding of the Nazi Party, after Hitler's release.

February 28
Friedrich Ebert, first President of the Weimar Republic, dies.

March 29   Presidential elections. The candi-
                     date supported by the Nazis, Luden-
                     dorff, receives only 211,000 of the
                     27 million votes cast.

April 26   Field Marshal Paul von Hindenburg
                     elected President in run-off elec-
                     tions.

Summer   Volume 1 of *Mein Kampf* published.

July 14   The occupying forces of the Ruhr
                     area begin their withdrawal.

October 5-16   Locarno Conference leads to reduc-
                     tion in tensions. Germany accepts
                     her Western borders, and receives
                     British and Italian guarantees for
                     them. Germany agrees not to use
                     force in changing her border toward
                     Poland.

October 22   German nationalist ministers leave
                     the government, as a protest against
                     the Locarno agreements.

1926
September 8   Germany admitted to the League of
                     Nations.

1928
May 20   Reichstag elections. Popular vote

for the Nazis 810,000 (2.6%), 12 seats in the 491-member house.

October 22   Hugenberg elected chairman of the German Nationalist Party, *Deutsch-nationale Volkspartei* (DNVP). He pursues a virulent nationalist policy of opposition to the foreign policy of the government.

1929

Hugenberg's huge publishing empire gives Hitler's speeches national coverage. Through Hugenberg, Hitler meets other industrialists and financiers who contribute to his campaign chest and to the Nazi Party.

June 30   Rhineland occupation by the Allies is terminated.

September   Hitler's and Hugenberg's joint fight in the "National Unity Front" against the acceptance of the Young Plan ends in defeat (4.1 million voices) but gains adherents for Hitler. Nazi voting support begins to increase.

1930

The world depression begins to affect Germany. Unemployment rises sharply and continues to increase rapidly.

March 29
Brüning (Center Party) appointed chancellor, to succeed Müller.

July 16
President Hindenburg invokes Article 48 of the Constitution, for emergencies: rule by presidential decree begins. The most influential people among the advisors of the President are Oskar von Hindenburg (his son), General von Schleicher, Otto Meissner (head of the presidential chancellery), Brüning, and von Papen.

September 14
Reichstag elections. The Nazis receive 6,409,600 votes (18.3%) and 107 seats in the 577-member house. The Nazi election campaign stresses overthrow of the Republic.

December
4.4 million unemployed.

1931-1932 Nazi Adherents Increase Steadily in Elections in the Various Länder.

1931

October 11
Harzburger Front, a union of Nazis, German Nationalist Party and *Stahlhelm* (Rightist paramilitary organization), is formed.

December   Germany has 5.66 million unem-
                  ployed.

1932
January 27   Hitler is invited to address the
                  powerful Industry Club to allay their
                  fears of the Nazis. He succeeds and
                  gets financial support from the Ruhr
                  industrialists.

March 13   Presidential elections. Hitler re-
                  ceives 11.5 million votes; Presi-
                  dent Hindenburg receives 18,661,736
                  votes. Since no candidate holds a
                  majority a run-off election is called.

April 10   Presidential elections. Hitler's pop-
                  ular vote increases to 13,417,460
                  (37%) but Hindenburg wins with a
                  clear majority of 19.25 million
                  votes.

April 14   Chancellor Brüning bans the Nazi
                  paramilitary units, the SA, the SS,
                  and their affiliated organizations,
                  as a danger to the state.

May 30   Chancellor Brüning replaced by von
                  Papen (German Nationalist Party).

June 16   The ban on the SA and the SS is
                  lifted by von Papen. Aggravation of

street fighting between Rightist and Leftist paramilitary groups.

July 20
Von Papen's coup d'état against the Socialist government in Prussia. Von Papen becomes Reich Commissar in Prussia.

July 31
Reichstag elections. The Nazis receive 13,745,800 votes (37.4% of the total votes cast). This gives them 230 seats in the 608-member house. The Nazis are now the largest single party in the Reichstag.

Nazi party membership increases from 100,000 in 1928 to ca. one million. Of these, 400,000 belong to the well-armed and disciplined SA and SS. The Reichswehr, by contrast, consists of 100,000 officers and men.

August 9
The government decrees the death penalty for political murder.

August 13
Hitler refuses to take the post of vice-chancellor in the von Papen cabinet.

November 6
Reichstag elections. Nazi popular vote reduced to 11,737,000 (33.1%

of the total votes cast). Their deputies are reduced to 196 of the 584
deputies.

December 2   General von Schleicher appointed
chancellor.

December 8   Crisis in the Nazi Party over the
conflict between Hitler and Gregor
Strasser, who resigns from his
offices in the Nazi Party.

1933
January 4   Von Papen and Hitler meet in the
home of the banker Schröder to dis-
cuss the formation of a new cabinet.

January 23   Chancellor von Schleicher resigns.

January 30   Hitler appointed chancellor, von
Papen vice-chancellor, and majority
of cabinet not Nazis.

February 22   40,000 SA and SS men sworn in as
auxiliary policemen.

February 27   The Reichstag building is burned.
Nazis accuse the Communists and
claim that Communists were about
to start an uprising.

February 28   Presidential decree gives Hitler

emergency powers, thus eliminating
basic civil rights and launching the
dictatorship. Reign of terror against
opponents. Establishment of SA concentration camps, mostly around
Berlin; almost all dissolved by
March 1934.

March 5
Reichstag elections. Despite an unlimited reign of terror and coercion
the Nazis fail to get a majority.
Popular vote: 17,277,200 (43.9% of
the total), 288 of 647 deputies. However, the German Nationalist Party
adds its 52 seats to those of the
Nazis, giving them a majority of 16.

March 13
Joseph Goebbels appointed Minister
for Popular Enlightenment and Propaganda.

The process of *Gleichschaltung* begins: Länder governments are dissolved and reconstituted according
to Reichstag elections. *Gleichschaltung* is the process of subduing all
political, economic and social life
so that it will be in step with Nazi
thought.

March 21
Special courts are established and
legislation for the prosecution of

political enemies *(Heimtückegesetz)* passed.

March 23   Enabling Act passed by the Reichstag and Reichsrat allows the government to rule by decree, until April 1937. Renewed in 1937.

April 1   National boycott of Jewish business and professional people.

April 7   Nazi federal commissioners appointed to run the Länder. Passage of *Reichsstatthaltergesetz* under which Nazi federal commissioners are appointed a month later to run the Länder.

May 1   First Four-Year-Plan announced.

May 2   The leaders of the labor unions are arrested and union headquarters are occupied by the Nazis. Instead of independent unions the *Deutsche Arbeitsfront* is created, headed by Robert Ley.

May 17   Strikes prohibited.

June 2   Beginning of public works program to reduce unemployment; *Autobahn* network to be built.

June 30   Laws to remove Jews and anti-
(April 7, July 20) Nazis from the legal profession and
                        the civil service.

July 14   NSDAP declared the only legal party.

August   SA and SS dismissed as auxiliary
                        police.

September 22   Reich Chamber of Culture estab-
                        lished, headed by Goebbels, to con-
                        trol press, music, theater, motion
                        pictures, and radio.

October 14   Withdrawal from League of Nations.

November 12   Reichstag elections. 95.2% of all
                        votes cast for Nazis; 661 deputies.

1934
January 26   Ten-year Non-Aggression Pact with
                        Poland.

January 30   Remaining autonomous powers of the
                        Länder abolished. Political *Gleich-*
                        schaltung thus completed, by the
                        elimination of federalism.

April   20   Reich Leader of the SS, Himmler,
                        appointed chief of the Prussian
                        Gestapo (Secret Police). Himmler

appointed head of all German police
forces on June 17, 1936.

June 17   Vice-chancellor von Papen speaks
at Marburg and denounces the
continuing Nazi revolution. He ex-
presses the fears of conservatives
and others.

June 30-July 2   Röhm purge. Röhm, chief of staff of
the SA and one of Hitler's friends,
murdered on Hitler's direct orders. Pretext: an imminent rising
of the SA; in fact, a sop to the
Reichswehr which was concerned
about the numbers and the power of
the armed SA, and elimination of
divergent social and political views
in the Nazi Party. Murders carried
out by squads of the *Leibstandarte*
Adolf Hitler. Also killed: General
von Schleicher and his wife, and
Kahr, whose body was found hacked
to pieces in a swamp near Dachau.
End of the influence of the SA, although some of it was restored at
the outbreak of war.

First official concentration camp
established in March 1933 at Dachau
near Munich. Subsequently the system was enlarged and administered

by the SS: 1936 Sachsenhausen (Oranienburg); 1937 Buchenwald; 1938 Flossenbürg; 1939 Ravensbrück (for women), and Mauthausen; 1940 Auschwitz I, Neuengamme, Natzweiler, and Gross-Rosen; 1942 Stutthof; 1943 Bergen-Belsen, and Mittelbau (Dora). In addition there were 406 labor camps attached to these camps. Until the beginning of World War II no more than 25,000 persons (except for the immediate aftermath of the pogrom of 1938) were imprisoned at any one time in concentration camps. By 1942 there were as many as 100,000 and by the end of the war 700,000 prisoners in German concentration camps.

July 25

Hitler-inspired putsch, by the Austrian Nazis, fails. Austrian Chancellor Dollfuss murdered.

August 2

President Hindenburg dies. The offices of chancellor and president are merged; Hitler becomes head of state (Führer and Reich Chancellor), and commander-in-chief of the armed forces. All officers and men take a personal oath to Hitler, not to the constitution as in the past.

August 19   Plebiscite on Hitler's new powers:
                  89.93% voted yes, 4.25 million voted
                  no.

1935
January 13   Saar votes overwhelmingly (90%) to
                  return to the Reich.

March 16   Conscription introduced to increase
                  armed forces to 550,000 men. (This
                  is a violation of the Versailles
                  Treaty.)

April 11   Great Britain, France, and Italy
                  meet at Stresa and condemn Hitler's
                  unilateral action. The Council of the
                  League of Nations censors Germany.

June 18   Anglo-German Naval Treaty. Lon-
                  don, unilaterally disregarding the
                  Versailles Treaty, agrees that Ger-
                  many may build her naval strength
                  up to 35% of British strength.

September   Nuremberg Laws against the Jews.
                  This entails, among other depriva-
                  tions of rights, loss of citizenship
                  and prohibition of intermarriage.
                  Jews made second-class citizens.

                  People's Courts are established with
                  the special authority to try cases of

treason; appeal possible only to Hitler.

1936

March 7   German troops occupy the demili-
                 tarized Rhineland. Hitler renounces
                 adherence to the Locarno Pact.

March 12   Great Britain, France, Italy and Bel-
                 gium denounce the German breach
                 of Locarno.

September   Second Four-Year-Plan announced;
                 Göring in charge of its execution.

November 6   Anti-Comintern Pact (Rome-Berlin
                 Axis) between Germany and Italy.

November 17   German-Japanese Pact: extension of
                 the Anti-Comintern Pact.

1937

November   Schacht resigns from Ministry of
                 Economics and a year later (Janu-
                 ary 1939) from the presidency of
                 the Reichsbank.

November 5   Hossbach Memorandum. (A historic
                 document, so-called because re-
                 cords of a secret military meeting
                 by Hossbach reveal Hitler's Grand
                 Design of Conquest.) Hitler declares

to his generals that Germany needs
territory, and Austria and Czechoslovakia should be conquered, pref-
erably in 1938, if the international
situation permitted such action.

1938 German Aggression against Austria and Czechoslovakia.

February 4

Dismissal of War Minister von
Blomberg and Army chief Fritsch.
Hitler takes over the supreme command of the armed forces. Ribbentrop is appointed Foreign Minister
in place of von Neurath.

March 12/13

Austria occupied. SS and Gestapo
terror immediately unleashed.

March 28

Hitler instructs Konrad Henlein, the
head of the Sudeten German Party
in Czechoslovakia, concerning his
future course of action.

May 20

Czechoslovakia orders partial mobilization.

May 30

Hitler orders execution of military
"Operation Grün"; plan to crush
Czechoslovakia, starting October 1.

September 12   Czechoslovakia declares martial law in its border areas.

September 15   British Prime Minister Chamberlain seeks peaceful settlement, arrives at Berchtesgaden to meet Hitler.

September 22   Chamberlain visits Hitler at Bad Godesberg.

September 29/30   Munich conference between France, Great Britain, Italy, and Germany.

September 30   The Munich Agreement provides that the bordering territory of Sudetenland is to be occupied by Germany. The German claim is based on the predominantly German population of Sudetenland.

October 1   Occupation of Sudetenland paves the way for depriving Czechoslovakia of her sovereignty. This area contains Czechoslovakia's major defenses against Germany.

November 9/10   Organized pogrom against the German Jews, ostensibly in "popular revenge" against the murder of a third secretary at the Paris embassy by a Polish Jew. Businesses

looted, synagogues burned, violence
in the form of killings and beatings,
and arrest of Jewish men to place
them in concentration camps.

1939 Beginning of World War II.

March 15

Occupation of the remainder of
Czechoslovakia. Creation of the
German protectorate of Bohemia and
Moravia, of Slovakia as a German
"protected" state; territory given to
Hungary and to Poland.

March 21

German occupation of Memel, a
German city given to Lithuania after
World War I.

March 31

Anglo-French guarantee to Poland.

April 11

"Case White," military operation
against Poland, prepared.

April 28

Germany cancels the Anglo-German
Naval Treaty and the German-Polish
Nonaggression Treaty.

May 22

German-Italian Pact of Steel signed.

May 23

Hitler tells his generals that war
with Poland is "inevitable."

June 14	Orders go out to the military staffs to complete plans for the attack on Poland by August 20.
June 22	Supreme Command of the Armed Forces (OKW) presents timetable to Hitler for the attack on Poland.
August 23	Nazi-Soviet Nonaggression Pact, with a secret agreement to divide Eastern Europe.
August 28	Hitler sets the hour for the invasion of Poland: 4:45 a.m. September 1.
September 1	Invasion of Poland, without a declaration of war.
September 3	Declaration of war against Germany by England and France.
September 17	Russian forces invade eastern Poland.
October 10	Operations in Poland declared completed.

1940

| April 9 | German invasion of Norway and Denmark. |

May 10   German invasion of Holland, Bel-
                   gium, Luxemburg, and France.

June 17   France requests armistice.

1941-1942

                   Extermination centers established
                   in Poland: Auschwitz II (Birkenau),
                   Belzec, Kulmhof, Maidanek (Lub-
                   lin), Sobibor, Trawniki, Treblinka.
                   Total victims: 3,000,000 – mostly
                   Jews from all over Europe. In addi-
                   tion, 2,100,000 Jews perished in
                   other places including 1,400,000 shot
                   and gassed by SS mobile units after
                   the invasion of Russia.

1941
April 6   Germany attacks Yugoslavia and
                   Greece.

June 22   German attack on the USSR.

1942
January 20   "Wannsee Conference": final deci-
                   sion to exterminate all of Europe's
                   Jews under the euphemism: "The
                   Final Solution of the Jewish Ques-
                   tion."

1943

January 31   German troops surrender at Stalin-
                     grad, thus sealing Germany's fate
                     in the Soviet Union.

1944

June 6   Allied invasion in France starts
                     ("D–Day").

July 20   Attempt on Hitler's life, and coup
                     by German anti-Nazi groups fails.
                     Thousands executed or imprisoned.

1945

April 30   Hitler commits suicide as Soviet
                     troops are taking Berlin.

May 7   German armies surrender uncon-
                     ditionally to the Allies at Rheims.